HE ANSWERED THE CALL
Coping with Our Loss—The Family's, Friends', and Firefighters' Perspectives

DC Firefighter Anthony Sean "Sauce" Phillips

The Fire on Cherry Road, NE

Lysa Phillips

Copyright © 2019 by Lysa Phillips.
All rights reserved. No part of this book may be reproduced in any form or by any electronic or mechanical means, including information storage and retrieval systems, without permission in writing from the publisher, except by a reviewer who may quote brief passages in a review.

Published by
LPS Marketing Designs, LLC

ISBN: 978-1-7339644-0-1
Second Printing, June 2019

Library of Congress Control Number: 2019904304

Book Cover and Interior Design by
Jessica Tilles of TWA Solutions and Services

Scriptures taken from the King James Version®. Copyright© 1982 by Thomas Nelson, Inc. Used by permission. All rights reserved.

The author has tried to recreate events, locales, and conversations from memories of them and interviews. To maintain anonymity, the author has changed some names and identifying details to protect the privacy of individuals.

For more information, contact lysa@lysaphillips.com.

Dedication

To our sons, Anthony, Jr. and Arzel Phillips, who have had to experience the tragic loss of their dad at such an early age. With God's covering and blessings over your lives, you have developed into fine, respectable, young men. You were your dad's pride and joy. At one time, he looked after you when you were in his presence, but now, he can keep watch over you wherever you are. Your dad and I are proud of you beyond measure.

To my loving daughter, Lyeah, who listened, sympathized, and prayed for and with us throughout the years; your words of encouragement helped us tremendously during our tough times.

Take Proverbs 3:5-6 on your journey through life: **"Trust in the Lord with all thine heart; and lean not unto thine own understanding. In all thy ways acknowledge him, and he shall direct thy paths."**

I LOVE YOU, ALWAYS!

Acknowledgments

A special thank you to...
Our beloved family and friends.

The men and women of the District of Columbia Fire and Emergency Medical Services Department for the planning, execution, and management of every detail of the memorial service and the funeral and their continued dedication to the family.

Fort Lincoln Cemetery for its contribution and dedication to delivering an unforgettable burial.

HEROES, Inc., for its general and educational financial support.

Former President Bill Clinton and First Lady Hilary Clinton and former Vice President Al Gore and other government officials for their phone calls and letters of condolences.

Former Washington, DC Mayor Anthony Williams, Washington, DC Congresswoman Eleanor Holmes Norton, Maryland Congressman Steny Hoyer, and Former Fire Chief Donald Edwards for their words of comfort and eulogy.

Former Captain John Burger and Lieutenant John Faulkner for their relentless work as the family's liaisons and going beyond the call of duty.

Bishop Oliver Subryan, Ebenezer Church of God, Hyattsville, Maryland, for always being available for the entire family.

International Association of Fire Fighters—Washington, DC Firefighters Association Local 36.

Former Deputy Fire Chief Edward Pearson for his continuous support of the family.

About the Author

A native of Grenada, West Indies—The Isle of Spice, Lysa Phillips wears many hats: mother, entrepreneur, marketing and design professional, and a woman of God. However, the one she cherishes the most is mother. Family and motherhood are the most important commitments in her life, raising three children over the last twenty-six years.

A graduate of Strayer University with a Bachelor of Business Administration in Marketing, with a minor in Human Resources, Lysa is the owner of LPS Marketing Designs, LLC, specializing in creative marketing and print graphic design solutions.

Of the many trials and tribulations Lysa has endured throughout her life, she is also challenged with a health condition that would alter her life forever. In 2003, Lysa was diagnosed with Lupus, an autoimmune illness that affects the organs and skin. Over the years, her struggle has not been easy, but she continues to persevere. She has been engaged and dedicated to spreading awareness, educate, and bring attention to the fight to end this illness by sharing her story, taking part in fundraising events, and partaking in online support groups. Her fight has become more critical after learning her daughter has the same illness.

Although Lysa is intuitive, with a gentle spirit, she is ambitious and leaves no stones unturned. Her strength, determination, family, and faith in God are the nucleus of her being.

Table of Contents

Foreword 1
Edward "Pete" Pearson
Retired Deputy Fire Chief–Operations

Introduction 5

Chapter 1 7
Who Was Anthony Sean "Sauce" Phillips?

Chapter 2 13
The Start of Our Lives Together

Chapter 3 23
The Initial Call into the Academy and His Rookie Experience at "The House of Pain"

Chapter 4 33
He Answered the Call, But It Didn't Seem Real

Chapter 5 42
The Fire on Cherry Road, NE

Chapter 6 65
Our Dad, the Hero

Chapter 7 83
The Difference He Made in Our Lives

Chapter 8 92
When One Is Hurt, We All Are Hurt…
When One Is Lost, We All Are Lost

Chapter 9 109
Celebrating the Life of a Man Who Lived for
God—Our Fallen Hero

Chapter 10 133
Coping After Everyone Has Moved On

Chapter 11 141
Planning for the Unavoidable

Conclusion 145

"A Soldier Gone Home" 148

In Memory Of 149

HE ANSWERED THE CALL
Coping with Our Loss—The Family's, Friends', and Firefighters' Perspectives

DC Firefighter Anthony Sean "Sauce" Phillips

The Fire on Cherry Road, NE

FOREWORD

A Line of Duty death in the fire service is a tragedy. It represents the loss of life of an individual who took an oath to protect the life and property of strangers.

In fire stations across the nation and abroad, men and women enter a profession with an inherent job description that requires placing their lives on the line for a stranger each time they answer a call for help. The tragedy is magnified when the Line of Duty death results from a firefighter performing the requirement of that inherent job description. This signals the firefighter has answered the "final call."

The fire service mourns the death of all firefighters who make the "supreme sacrifice," hailing them as heroes by fellow firefighters and those outside the profession. The devastation of a Line of Duty death, in every instance, carries personal grief for the family and friends of the firefighters, as often they are husbands, wives, fathers, and mothers, along with inherent roles of daughters, sons, sisters, and brothers.

Lysa is the wife of a firefighter who made the supreme sacrifice. On May 30, 1999, Anthony "Sauce" Phillips answered the call to a house fire on Cherry Road in Washington, DC, as a proud member of Engine Company 10, known throughout the fire service as "The House of Pain." Anthony left behind a wife, a six-year-old son, Lil' Tony, and a twenty-one-month-old son, Arzel.

I served as Sauce's officer at Engine 10 after transferring/moving across the floor from Truck Company 13. He was on the line when Engine 10 encountered a basement fire on Gales Street, which left me with second-degree burns to my face, chin, and neck. Upon returning to duty, I accepted an assignment at the training academy. His supreme sacrifice occurred ten months after I left The House of Pain.

Lysa's story of survival required her to encounter the fire service tacit knowledge—"deeply embedded cultural beliefs which are thought to be in a culture's way of seeing the world, to the point that they are never discussed by members of the culture and must be picked up by the writer," which she did. Her faith in God proved instrumental in accepting her husband answering the call. His ultimate sacrifice allowed me to re-dedicate my life to God as I returned to the church of his homegoing service the following Sunday and became a faithful member for the next sixteen years.

Lysa shares her story of life with her hero up to his supreme sacrifice in an impactful and spiritual manner, which provides a model for survival in the aftermath of the "Line of Duty" death of a husband and father. A testament of her survival is seen in their sons—Tony, as he is called today, having dropped the Lil' soon after his dad made the supreme sacrifice, and Arzel, who doesn't recall much, but has embraced the little time he had with his dad. They both are now proud, successful young men who honor and greatly admire the heroism and legacy of the late DC Firefighter Anthony Sean "Sauce" Phillips.

Edward "Pete" Pearson
Retired Deputy Fire Chief–Operations
DC Fire and EMS Department

INTRODUCTION

*T*wo dead and three sustained injuries ranging from critical to minor. That was the outcome of a response to an early morning call of a basement fire in a townhouse on Cherry Road, NE, in Washington, DC, on May 30, 1999.

My late husband, DC Firefighter Anthony "Sauce" Phillips, who served at Engine 10, known as "The House of Pain" and the "busiest engine company in the nation," perished in the line of duty at the young age of thirty. Known to family and friends as Tony and "Sauce" to his fellow firefighters, he had only served three years in the department after a seven-year wait to achieve his dream of becoming a DC firefighter before going home to be with the Lord while "doing his job," to serve, protect, and save the lives in the community.

Personnel interviewed after the incident stated that they considered the alarm to be a "routine" call. Yet, this fire claimed the lives of two firefighters: Anthony Phillips and Louis Matthews, a seven-year veteran from Engine Company 26. Firefighter Joe Morgan, an eight-year veteran from Engine Company 26, sustained second- and third-degree burns to sixty percent of his body. Lieutenant Charles Redding, a seventeen-year veteran from Engine Company 26, sustained second-degree burns to his face, hands, and back. Firefighter Stanley Taper, a seven-year veteran from Engine Company 12, suffered minor injuries.

He Answered the Call: Coping with Our Loss—The Family's, Friends', and Firefighters' Perspectives shares the real-life, sensitive story about Anthony "Sauce" Phillips by those who loved him and those who worked beside him, sharing their struggles of his passing, how it impacted them, and the mechanisms they used to cope over the years.

Losing a loved one is traumatic, whether a family member or a friend. Losing them in the line of duty, with no warning, can be even more detrimental. It is also an overwhelming, frightening, and painful experience. Those left to mourn often find themselves in a complex web of emotions. Although death is beyond our control, the wonderful memories left behind can shine the light on how such a tragedy can transform into a testimony for others as they cope with their loss.

CHAPTER One

Who was Anthony Sean Phillips?

A gift from God to mankind, Anthony Sean Phillips was born on October 19, 1968, in the District of Columbia, to Wydenia "Dee" Cook and Joseph Phillips. Dee, a young mother, lived at home with her parents where she nurtured Tony. About thirteen months later, Tony became a big brother to his sibling, Melvin. Dee later met and married Leon Saunders (deceased). Together, they raised Tony and Melvin into fine young men. Many years later, he and Melvin became big brothers to their sister, Dominique.

Like many teenage boys, Tony and Melvin enjoyed playing sports and had quite a few friends with whom they enjoyed hanging out. Tony was a likable and easy-going person, who got along well with others. At fourteen years old, he and his mother joined Bethesda New Life Gospel Church where he fellowshipped with young people his age

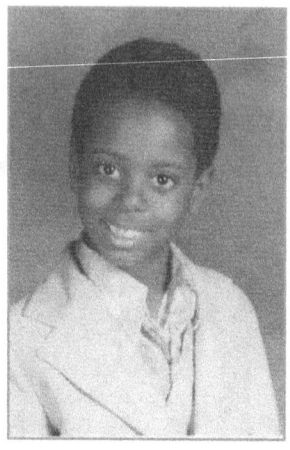
Tony as a youth.

and learned from those who were older. Being amongst God-fearing people, who provided him with spiritual guidance, prompted him to serve the Lord with songs by joining the Youth Chorus.

In 1988, Tony completed his high school education and graduated from Theodore Roosevelt High School in Washington, DC. That was an exciting time for him and his parents. He'd done it! He graduated!

As a young man who always tried to stay on course, he did the same in his walk with Christ. Because of his spiritual nurturing through the Word of God, Tony desired to serve in other capacities within the church and later joined the Usher Board.

Even though Tony loved the Lord and lived a Christian life, his appreciation for DC's most popular music—Go-Go—was close to his heart, second to God. He *loved* this subgenre, associated with funk music, that originated in the area during the mid-sixties to late-seventies. Tony and his friends were avid followers of Go-Go. It coursed through their veins. Wherever Rare Essence, Chuck Brown and the Soul Searchers, and other bands were playing, The Late-Night Crew was there, too. The Late-Night Crew was what Tony and his friends called themselves. Because they were followers of the music and the bands, the artists would shout out "The Late-Night Crew" during performances—many recorded live.

As I grew stronger in my faith, I prayed that Tony's faith would increase. He loved the Lord, but Go-Go was always in him. I would ask him to limit the time he spent at the Go-Go. I wanted him to spend more time in church, nurturing his relationship with God. And, he did.

Tony (far right) and his friends at the Go-Go.

It didn't take long for him to commit more time to God. He attended church and worked within other ministries, including singing with the Kings of Faith, working with the young men in the Men's Fellowship Ministry, and serving as a percussionist, a trustee, and the president of the Audio/Visual Ministry. Soon, he attended church more than he attended the Go-Go. Tony was working for the Lord now. I knew once he committed himself more to the Lord that God would bless him with his desires.

The Tony I met in 1989 and had grown to know and marry, was a man who had a calmness about him, which was one of his many qualities that attracted me. He had extreme humility; one who saw the best in and brought the best out of everyone he met. His positive energy was contagious. Something about him made me want to hold on to him, hoping to build a future together. He had the spirit of God all over him that shined bright. He was caring, loving, and giving; he always kept me in stitches, laughing at his subtle jokes. He joked on a whim; you never saw it coming. Tony kept me grounded and helped me through many tough times in my life as a young woman. He was my confidant, and I could always talk to him and depend on him to give me his best advice. He had my best interest at heart and always kept a positive attitude. There was no downtime when Tony was around; his presence lifted spirits.

Besides his love for Go-Go, he had an equal amount of love playing Madden NFL 99 on the PlayStation circuit with his friends. Their commitment to playing the game became competitive, which led to annual tournaments. There were long nights of Madden at any of their homes every week. One day, I got upset with him because of the time he was spending playing the game and returning home late. I told him I would lock him out of the house if he didn't stop coming in at such early hours in the morning. As clever as he was, the next time he went to game night, he took Lil' Tony with him to make sure I didn't follow through on that threat. That was Tony; he was very crafty. There was no way I could have stayed upset with him; he wouldn't allow it.

30th birthday limousine ride.

Who was Anthony Sean Phillips? He was a son, brother, father, husband, friend, firefighter, and a man of God. Known to many, those who held him dear to their hearts gave him aliases, but fellow firefighters knew him as "Sauce." To his mother, he was Pookie. To his church family, he was Moses. To his fellow bowlers, he was Twinkle Toes. He was never a follower of man. He lived a life for God, which spoke volumes for him. The outpouring from people who did not know him, but felt the hurt and pain of his passing, was a validation of his God-fearing spirit. People from all walks of life lined the streets of Washington, DC, on June 4, 1999, mourning him as Engine 10's fire truck carried his casket to his final resting place. The daily news coverage leading up to his funeral was unlike anything I had ever seen; something befitting of a hero who died in the line of duty.

The expressions of love showed the life he lived as an imitator of God. Anthony Sean Phillips' light shined before others who saw his good works, giving glory and honor to his Father in heaven.

CHAPTER Two

The Start of Our Lives Together

*I*n life, there are moments you forget and then there are those that will stay with you forever. The moment he walked through that door is a memory that will stay with me for my lifetime.

It was in 1989, on a Saturday evening. I was working as a cashier at Popeyes Louisiana Kitchen on New Hampshire Avenue in Takoma Park, Maryland. When I laid eyes on him, I knew he would be my future husband. Although I was sixteen years old, I had instinct. I claimed it. I knew it. So, it would be.

Like most teenage girls, I was interested in boys. Astounded by his brown eyes, wavy hair, chocolate complexion, and the nice herringbone gold necklace around his neck, I wanted him to step into my line and hoped that I wouldn't get tongue-tied. He did. It elated me. Tickled pink was more like it. I was nervous, which was unusual for me. Meeting or having conversations with boys came easy for me, so I couldn't understand why I was experiencing so much anxiety. His name was Tony. He was with one of his boys. They both were cute, but I had my sights on Tony. It was more than his outside appearance I found appealing and piqued my interest; I believe it was the spirit of God that surrounded him. His demeanor and his presence seemed so gentle and real.

When he stepped up to my register for me to take his order, I wore the biggest smile. In my soft-spoken voice, I asked, "Welcome to Popeyes, may I take your order?" He gave me his order while joking with me, making me laugh. He was also very charming. Joy bubbled inside me; I was so excited. My heart pitter-pattered. As I turned around to fix his order, I overheard him and his friend behind me, discussing which one would give me their number. I wanted and took Tony's. It seemed like he was as excited for me to take his number as I was getting it. Aside from all the other numbers in my pocket I'd collected that day from other boys, I couldn't wait for my shift to end so I could get home to call him. I had an instant crush on Tony. A crush that, over the years, never faded.

At the end of my shift, I called him when I got home.

"Do you have a girlfriend?" was the first question that tumbled out of my mouth.

"No, but I have a girl I'm intimate with right now. Just let me see her one more time."

Though he gave a bold response, he was honest, which was a trait I appreciated. We talked several times during the week, and he often visited Popeyes during my shifts. I remember joking with him about what he liked more, the chicken or me.

The Start of Our Lives Together

Over time, Tony and I had gotten to know each other better. Even with the four-year age gap, we got along well and had wonderful conversations about any and everything under the sun. I fell for him. He fell for me. Soon, we found ourselves in that comfort zone of being a couple and becoming a part of the "couple mix" with his friends and their girls. We had done so much together as young couples do—going places and to events—even wearing shirts inscribed with each other's names. He even let me wear his jewelry. During that time, it was a big thing for a girl to wear her boyfriend's chain. It meant exclusivity.

Tony and me as a young couple.

We learned so much about each other and had often shared our goals and desires. He shared his longing to become a firefighter. He had taken the exam and was waiting to hear from the department. He felt so adamant about becoming a firefighter; so much that he only accepted flexible jobs in the meantime, because he expected that call to come through soon. While waiting on that call, he worked as a courier for different companies. He waited and waited…

The time had come when he wanted me to meet his mother. Oh my, I wasn't sure if I was ready for that; but I met her, and I'm glad I did. She was an evangelist in their church, Bethesda New Life Gospel Church, in northeast Washington, DC. Being a nervous wreck and somewhat intimidated, I didn't know how to address her—Ms. Saunders, Ms. Dee, or Evangelist. So, I settled on, "Hello." During my time conversing with her, I never referred to her by name or anything else. I was hoping she would tell me how to address her, but she didn't, so I responded without using her name. Can you imagine how difficult that was? It was my first time ever having to get so close to a boyfriend's mother to engage in a one-on-one conversation. We had a very pleasant exchange. But, as a mother who seemed to be protective of her son, I couldn't tell how she felt about me. However, meeting her opened the door for me to visit Tony at his home without fear.

After meeting his mom, I knew Tony would one day expect me to visit his church. I think he knew his mother would invite me. Well, he was right; she did just that. How could I say no, and why would I? I accepted the invitation. This was perfect because I was looking for a church home. Raised with Christian values and attempting to live a Christian life, I frequented my mother's church, but wanted to find a church and a church family I could call my own.

After my first visit to Bethesda New Life Gospel Church, I knew this was where I wanted to be, where I knew I could continue to grow in my faith. I felt the love and compassion from the members, but, in particular, from Reverend Iola B. Cunningham. She had a Holy glow around her that exuded her anointing, her love for Christ. It was clear the spirit of God was abundant through her.

At seventeen, I joined the church. As I became more knowledgeable about the Word of God and the Christian principles and teachings, I surrendered my life to Christ. Tony was very encouraging and happy to see the changes in my life. At eighteen years old, I experienced a spiritual cleansing by baptism. To be so young, choosing a church home and baptism were two of the best and most important decisions I had made. Look at God! I attribute all those blessings to God placing Tony in my life.

During my senior year of high school, I was part of the work-study program where I attended school for a half day and worked at Sovran Bank, now Bank of America, the other half. I knew I wanted to attend college and work in corporate America. During that year, several students, whose academics qualified them, could receive a full scholarship to the University of Maryland University College by submitting the most exceptional essay, detailing why they were deserving of the scholarship. I had excellent grades, met the academic qualifications, and I wanted to attend college, so I jumped on board. Several weeks later, I learned I received a scholarship. Oh my gosh—I was going to college! I was so elated. The first person I shared the great news with was Tony. He was excited for me also, and repeated what he'd always said, "I've got a smart girl."

In May 1991, Tony escorted me to my prom and attended my graduation in June. We were inseparable. As it goes with most relationships, his friends felt a certain way because he was spending so much time with me. They called me "that Jamaican girl," even though I am Grenadian. And, for whatever reason, anyone who hailed from the Islands or the Caribbean, with an accent, was a Jamaican. As a couple, Tony and I grew closer, and I knew I wanted to have a future with him.

Several months after graduating high school, I learned I was with child. I contacted Tony and, shaking with fear and in tears, I shared the news with him.

"I don't know what to do. I am not ready to be a mother."

He didn't appear as devastated nor as afraid as I was. In fact, he was thrilled.

"You are having my son. You are having my son!"

Out of his crew of friends, I believe he was the first one to have a child. He was over the moon. Yet, I felt apprehensive. I

Tony and me, pregnant with Lil' Tony.

had given my life to Christ and now it was clear I had sinned. It concerned Tony and me about what the members of the church would think and what our parents would say or how they would react. I had a scholarship, and I was getting ready to start a new job at Geico in Chevy Chase, Maryland. To say I was unprepared was an understatement.

It was scary sharing the news with my mother. I convinced Tony we would have separate conversations with our parents. Neither of our parents took it well, but at least they didn't kill us. We didn't want to wait until the pregnancy was visible to surprise our church family, so we shared the news with some.

We were members of a church that held Christians accountable for their walk with Christ. It was no different for Tony and me. After the elders learned about the results of our iniquities, I feared what they would say, or if they would chastise us. However, that wasn't the case. They expressed their disappointment in how we didn't do things the way God has orchestrated it in His Word—marriage before intimacy—but they didn't condemn us. Instead, Tony and I had to go before the elders to confess our wrongs, as other couples in similar situations had to do in the past. This was a biblical practice of the church, as noted in James 5:16, *"Therefore confess your sins to each other and pray for each other so that you may be healed. The prayer of a righteous person is powerful and effective."*

More frightened than Tony, I trembled and cried through the entire confession. The elders embraced us and showed us lots of love and support, which warmed my heart and lessened my fear and the disappointment I held within myself. Tony, as it was in all circumstances, kept equanimity during the entire fiasco. That was just like him—allowing nothing to bother him.

A few months later, Tony proposed. It wasn't anything fancy. He didn't get down on one knee. There was no lobster meal. However, it was a surprise. We were standing outside his parents' home, fussing. I don't recall what the disagreement was about, but he pulled out a ring.

"See? All I want to do is marry you!"

That's how it happened. He gave me the ring and shut me up. A huge smile and excitement replaced whatever caused the disagreement.

"Are you serious?"

"Yeah." He smiled.

I felt like Shug Avery in *The Color Purple*: "I's getting married!" Although we had put the cart before the horse, I felt things would be all right and done right. The cart was now following the horse.

In June 1992, I was nineteen and Tony was twenty-three. We welcomed our nine-pound-seven-ounce baby boy into the world. Already set for his firstborn, Tony had decided on the name Arzel Shamar Phillips, but I convinced him to give his firstborn his name as a junior. He agreed to name him Anthony Sean Phillips, Jr. It was one of the proudest days of his life. He had his son! I told him we would hold on to the original name for his second-born son.

We had to step it up. We were parents now. I was working a full-time job, attending college at night, living with my parents; and as a new mother, learning how to care for our precious baby, while Tony was working full time and learning the skill of fatherhood. He was amazing, as we worked things out with the help and support of our family. I will admit, the responsibilities were challenging, but we hung in there and continued to strive.

A little more than a year later, on December 10, 1993, we became husband and wife. On that day, the church was having a vow renewal ceremony, and since we were building our little family and didn't have a lot of money to spend on a wedding, we had our ceremony right after the vow renewal. We planned it with the help of several leaders of the church, who had our best interests at heart and wanted us to succeed. It was also a huge surprise for the church members attending the renewal ceremony. They had no clue what was happening when our family and the wedding party flowed into the church. We had an intimate reception in the fellowship hall with our families, friends, and the couples who renewed their vows. It was a

The Start of Our Lives Together

Just married.

special day for us as we united alongside those who had shared a long-lasting love with one another in marriage.

We were married! I was twenty years old, a wife and a mother. Tony was twenty-four years old, a husband and a father! Although we were young, we knew with God and with the support of our family and friends, we would be okay.

After the ceremony, my mom suggested that Tony, the baby, and I live with her until we could afford our own place. Plus, I knew she didn't want her grandson to be away from her. Tony and I discussed it and didn't hesitate to accept the offer. We knew it would give us time to save more money so we could be in a better financial position to move forward. Look at us, we were making our first decision as husband and wife!

We lived with my parents for three months before moving into our first apartment. For the first time in both our lives, we were on our own. We were a family, learning how to be husband and wife, living together, and building a family structure. Although we had no experience and no manual to follow, filled with adventure, we were ready for the journey to learn and grow. We held on to our faith and the support and guidance from those who loved us as we moved forward in that phase of our lives together.

CHAPTER Three

The Initial Call into the Academy and His Rookie Experience at "The House of Pain"

In October 1995, after seven years of waiting, Tony received his appointment to the DC Fire Recruit Training Academy to undergo the first phase of becoming a DC firefighter. Yes! God had opened the door for him and blessed him with his desire. Words could not express the overwhelming excitement he felt. At long last, his dream was manifesting.

The training process was difficult. It challenged his physical and mental capabilities, but he never wavered; and with his strong faith in God, he made it through. It delighted us to attend the graduation on March 22, 1996, to see him accept the Certificate of Completion, and take the Firefighter Oath, about which he was serious and passionate.

To share a little history, firefighters fall under the Constitution's Article VI as members of the Executive Branch of government sworn to uphold the public's trust. The constant threat of fire was at the forefront of protecting our communities in the New World. No one could fight the fire alone, so for their general welfare, the colonists organized early fire companies. In 1773, Ben Franklin, the father of the American Fire Service, wrote under a pen name, "Soon after it [a fire] is seen and cry'd out, the place is crowded by active men of different ages, professions, and titles who, as of one mind and rank, apply themselves with all vigilance and resolution, according to their abilities, to the hard work of conquering the increasing fire."[1]

Tony was now a DC Firefighter, promising to defend the Constitution of the United States. While each jurisdiction's oath may vary, they all contain the substantive language that everyone shall "uphold the Constitution, faithfully and impartially discharge the duties, and obey the laws of this state and city," of which Tony promised to do with honor. That was a proud day for him and our family.

Many new recruits graduating from the training academy during that time wanted to go to Engine 10, because it was, and still is, the busiest engine company in the United States. Engine 10 is one of thirty-three engine companies in the District of Columbia and is one of thirty-four paramedic units

---

[1] Ricci, Frank and Shestokas, David, "Understanding the Fire Service Oath You are Promising to Uphold," *Fire Rescue Magazine,* June 6, 2018, www.firerescuemagazine.com.

The Initial Call into the Academy and His Rookie Experience at "The House of Pain"

After graduation from the training academy.

in operation. It receives an average of four hundred fifty calls a month, and while most calls are medical, it still receives one to two fires per week.[2] That was Tony's assignment: Engine 10. Known as "The House of Pain," Engine 10 provides rookies with the needed experience to become a great firefighter. Since Tony "came off the street," as he did not attend the cadet program, he had no formal, extensive field experience. Therefore, he believed Engine 10 would be the perfect place for him—a young man anxious and motivated to do what he had been longing to do and what God had called him to do.

Some of Tony's fellow firefighters have shared many funny memories with me and the not-so-favorable experiences. One, in particular, which seemed to be an across-the-board memory for them all, was Tony's first day at Engine 10. He arrived with "Hot Sauce" inscribed on his jacket. Learning that rookies received a nickname, he didn't wait for them to come up with one for him. He had his own already in place. A lover of hot sauce, he felt that should be his firehouse nickname. Firefighters tried to explain to him the tradition of how rookies received their nicknames. It was not up to the rookie to come up with a nickname. That was the sole responsibility of the other firefighters in the house or on their shift, which made no difference to him. That's the name he wanted. Not agreeing with him, they called him all kinds of sauce-related names and more. They settled on "Sauce."

---

[2] Pakken, John, "What Happens When You Call 911 in Washington, DC," *Washingtonian*, February 1, 2009. https://www.washingtonian.com/2009/02/01/what-happens-when-you-call-911-in-washington-dc/

*The Initial Call into the Academy and His Rookie
Experience at "The House of Pain"*

Fellow firefighter, Kwame Roberts, remembers Tony entering Engine 10 as an energetic, young rookie, eager to learn and hit the ground running. After a while, he noticed a change in his vitality and desire. Tony didn't feel as comfortable and accepted as he thought he would be, coming in as a rookie. "We saw each other in the mornings, during a shift change," said Roberts. "That's when we would have our hour-long conversations." He noted that Tony, the only African American on his shift, told him he felt isolated, racially targeted, and received unfair treatment from his officers and co-firefighters, which was noticeable by other firefighters. He expressed Tony's frustration; he wanted a transfer to another station that was not predominantly Caucasian. "It was obvious what he was going through, but I explained to him that if he wanted to be here, 'Don't let anyone discourage you and try to get you out. You let them know that this is your city, you grew up here, and they are coming into your community. And if they want to get you out, tell them they will have to work harder than that to do so.'"

The harassment and teasing were having a negative impact on Tony and his drive to function, learn, and fulfill his duties as a DC firefighter. This was the main reason he wanted a transfer, but his officer also wanted him transferred. "I believe Tony became so enraged, he felt like he could physically hurt them," said Roberts.

Even with the struggles, Tony endured. Encouragement from an African American captain from another engine company and other firefighters gave him added confidence and strength to withstand. He was eager to learn how to deal with racism in a civilized manner, which led him to study the

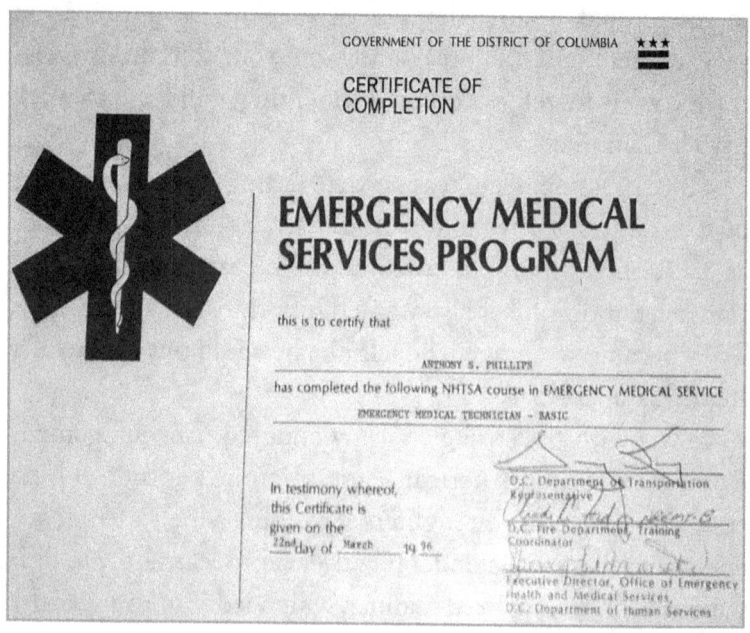

The Initial Call into the Academy and His Rookie Experience at "The House of Pain"

various teachings of Dr. Martin Luther King, Jr. and Malcolm X. Tony did not allow racism to deter him from learning the skills necessary to do the job well. He prevailed through the negativity and focused on his calling.

Still, after his probationary period, Tony was ready to transfer to Engine 30. "I first learned from the battalion chief of a probationary trainee who was ready to leave 10 Engine to get to 30 Engine, once he fulfilled his probationary requirement," said retired Deputy Fire Chief Edward Pearson (former lieutenant from Engine 10). "I introduced myself to the guys and I knew exactly who the guy was. It was Tony Phillips." Pearson told me he knew Tony was the one because "It was obvious; he was the only African American on that shift." As Engine 10 is "The House of Pain," Engine 30, then was the "Dirty 30," with "The Soul Train" inscribed on the fire truck. Engine 30 is predominately African American.

Still, Tony battled with the differential treatment when it came to race, and he was passionate about saving and protecting lives. "I had asked Tony to come into my office," said Pearson. "I said to him, 'Chief told me you put your papers in to be transferred. Why do you want to leave?'

'I just don't like the way they treat my people,' he said.

'What do you mean, how they treat your people?'

'When it's a fire call, they break their necks to get on that fire truck. But when the call is dispatched for a medical emergency, they take their time. And, when we go to calls in the middle of the night for sick people, they are a little disgruntled because it broke their sleep. I don't like that. I can't be around that. I like the guys, but I can't stay here while they treat my people like this.'

"At that point, I could relate to him," Pearson continued, "because I had been assigned to Engine 6, which was in the late eighties, and there was a lot of racial tension there.

"I suggested we make a pack. 'I want you to stay here with me for thirty days and if you still feel like you want to transfer, then I'm fine with it, but give me thirty days to work with you.'

'Well, I've had officers and all…they can't change these guys and I don't think you're going to be able to change them either.'

'Give me my thirty days and let's see.'

"I did make some initiatives that weren't taken too lightly by the guys initially, but in the long run, they realized…it was almost like they had gotten away with a lot of things for a long time, and now they had an officer that wasn't going to accept inequality, especially where he grew up. I am a native Washingtonian. Tony was, too. So, I shared it with him and started making changes in the way we did things that didn't reflect the guys being insensitive to the community. After those thirty days were up—actually, I don't think it was quite thirty days—Tony and I were standing outside of 10 Engine, about two in the morning.

'Hey, still wanna go to 30 Engine?' I asked him.

He busted out laughing and said, 'Yeah, right. Only if you're going.'

'I ain't going.'

'Well, I ain't going either.'"

Tony stayed with Engine 10, thanks to the amazing leader and mentor, Lieutenant Edward Pearson.

*The Initial Call into the Academy and His Rookie
Experience at "The House of Pain"*

And, amid all of this, I came home one day after work and told him I was ready to have another child. He looked at me, laughed, and said, "Who have you been talking to?"

"No one. I think I am ready for another child."

It didn't take long. Several months later, I was pregnant with our second child. Our son, Arzel Shamar Phillips, was born in August 1997. Tony gave his second-born son the name he had for his firstborn, as I promised him. The joy of having another son took away from the issues he faced on the job. It also motivated him to keep forging ahead because he had to provide for a wife and, now, two sons.

Tony differed greatly from many young men his age. He was a laid-back individual, who refused to let anything or anyone hold him back. He didn't allow many things to bother him. His character and faith in God kept him focused and determined to accomplish. He could be in an environment with various types of people, doing various things, and not fall prey to what was going on around him. He would not take part in activities if it was not of God or if it compromised his character. Many of his fellow firefighters shared that he never involved himself in some of their actions, like cursing, drinking, smoking, negative conversations, or such things that would show him in a negative light, which only proved his Christian nature.

"We always enjoyed having Tony work with us," said John Faulkner, Firefighter, Engine 10. "He fitted in with our shift just great. However, I had the feeling Tony was the type to get along with just about everyone."

Tony continued to work hard and proved that firefighting was his calling. "What people need to understand," said

Firefighter James "Gordo" Gordon, who was at Engine 10 in 1999 as Tony's shift relief, "is that Tony came off the street with no experience and was thrown into the busiest firehouse in the country. So, during his time there, he gained more experience than someone with twenty years."

Tony knew God's purpose for his life was to serve the community. Therefore, he did not allow racist words, unfair treatment, and other distractions imposed upon him to force him to give up. Rather, it motivated him to push through the pandemonium. A man of God, Tony knew when you are working to fulfill God's Will, the enemy will place stumbling blocks in your way by using others as distractions to hold you back. However, the spiritual strength Tony owned, and with God guiding his footsteps, he fulfilled his duties as a DC firefighter.

Job well done, Firefighter Phillips!

CHAPTER Four

He Answered the Call, But It Didn't Seem Real

"Hey, babe, do you mind if I go in to do some overtime?"

That was the question Tony asked me on the evening of Friday, May 28, 1999, after he received a call from Engine 10 with the request to work extra hours. Of all holidays, Memorial Day weekend is a tough weekend for firefighters worldwide and it is no different at Engine 10. Having as many "hands on deck" as possible is a must.

"That's fine," I told him. "We can always use the extra money."

It was just a regular Friday evening, and we didn't have major plans.

The next day around noon, the boys and I got ready and left the house, heading to the church for Lil' Tony's choir rehearsal. Our church was not too far from Engine 10. Plus, that day was Big Tony's shift to work.

I did something we never did. I asked the boys, "Do you want to go to the firehouse to visit Daddy?"

"Yeah," they responded in unison.

It was rare for us to visit the firehouse, so it thrilled the boys. Engine 10 is the busiest engine company for a reason. However, I had a strong feeling about doing a quick visit that day, though I didn't know why.

After rehearsal, we drove down to the firehouse, got out of the vehicle, and knocked on the side door. If I recall correctly, Firefighter K. Roberts opened the door to let us in. Tony was thrilled to see us. The boys ran up to him and embraced him as if they had not seen him in a long time. It didn't take long before Tony's fellow firefighters got involved with playing with the boys, taking photos on the firetruck and sliding down the pole. It was the time of their lives, enjoying their time with their dad at work. And, too, I'm sure being inside the firehouse was so exciting for two little boys. It was ironic that the Lord laid it on my spirit to go down to the firehouse that day.

After fifteen minutes into our visit, the call bell blared—Daddy had to go. Rushing to prepare to answer the call, Big Tony yelled out, "Babe, we got to go," as he walked us out in haste. He gave us a hug and a kiss and placed Arzel in his car seat. As he ran back to the fire truck, I yelled out, "I will cook tonight so I won't have to do it tomorrow; and when you come home in the morning, we will be prepared for church," and off he went to respond to the call.

Around two o'clock in the morning on Sunday, May 30, 1999, as I lay in my bed with my two children beside me, I

He Answered the Call, But It Didn't Seem Real

Lil' Tony and Arzel at Engine 10 on May 29, 1999, the night before their dad died.

received a phone call. The male voice on the other end of the phone said, "Hello, Mrs. Phillips, please open your door. We have information on your husband."

Waking up out of my sleep in a daze, I thought one of his friends was joking around with me. The person repeated the same information. I don't remember if the person claimed to be DC Fire Department Chaplain or if it was the individual with him. At that moment, visions of a military representative standing at the front door to inform the family of the loss of their loved one jolted me out of bed.

I walked down the steps to the door and opened it. A firefighter and a chaplain walked toward me. The chaplain approached with outstretched arms, telling me, "I'm sorry." I backed away from the door and moved toward the kitchen. I knew why they were there. The indescribable emotions that racked my insides; I felt sick. For the first time in my life, I felt grief like nothing I'd ever felt before.

As tears streamed down my face, the first thing I could muster was, "How could you come to my house to tell me this? What will happen to our boys?"

I thought of nothing else but how this tragedy would destroy the children. How were they going to handle the loss of their daddy? He was their world, as they were his. As those words came out of my mouth, it felt like someone wrapped their arms around me and I felt peace course through me, traveling from head to toe. A calmness, in which I had never experienced in my life. But those were not human arms. The Spirit of the Lord was present to hold and comfort me as referenced in Philippians 4:7, **"And the peace of God, which passeth all understanding, shall keep your hearts and minds through Christ Jesus."**

In my next breath, I told the chaplain, "I need to contact my mother and my pastor."

"You are a woman of great faith," he said.

Then, everything went blank.

After contacting my mother, I called my brother, Hayden, to inform him about Tony and to ask him to come over to stay with the children so I could go to Washington Hospital Center.

The chaplain, firefighter, and I traveled to the hospital. It felt like the longest ride of my life. We entered through a back entrance. John Burger, who was the captain of Engine 10 then, was there to meet me.

"When I got to the hospital," said Burger, "no one had shown up yet. I talked to the charge nurse, telling her who I was, and that family was coming in. I wanted to try to keep everybody occupied and to give them as much information as possible, so I needed to know what was going on. Tony was deceased, Lou Matthews was in surgery, and Joe Morgan was in surgery. I got as much information as I could and waited to see who would show up.

"He [Tony] was badly burned because it hit him in the face. They tried to intubate him, by putting a tube in his throat; it had scorched his face and throat. They worked on him, but by the time they got him to the hospital, they pronounced him dead at 1:08 a.m. I needed to see him before Lysa got to the hospital. He still had the air tube sticking out of his mouth. And so, I said to the nurse, 'Can we take that out of his mouth?' and she said, 'No, we cannot take that out because the coroner will want to see if it was put in correctly.' So, I asked her, 'Can we at least cut it off below his lips so we can hide it?' She just looked at me: and I said, 'His wife is coming in and we can't have her seeing that.' It was hard enough to see how swollen he was. So, she [nurse] was good about that. I kind of helped her. I thanked her because it was choking me looking at him that way.

"I dialed Edwards, who was the fire chief, and he showed up. I gave him a quick brief of what I'd found out and he would wait to greet the family members when they showed up. Joe Morgan's mother and his fiancé were first to show up. I introduced them to the fire chief, and they went off to the side.

"Then, at that point, Lysa arrived. I explained things to her. She wanted to see Tony, but I said, 'I don't know if you really want to do this at the moment…' But she wanted to see him."

Still in shock and disturbed, Burger escorted me to a room where my husband and the father of my children lay flat on his back on a hospital gurney, with his arms resting still at his sides, his eyes closed.

When I looked at my husband, I found the strength to say, "This is not my husband. This is just a shell." I knew the Lord had already secured the soul of His devoted steward. He looked as if he was asleep.

For as long as I live… That's how long I will have the vision of my husband—on a metal gurney, dead. It continues to play back in my mind—my heart bleeds, my heart hurts, my heart aches—my husband, the father of my children was gone. Now, what was I supposed to do? How was this going to affect our children? *Lord, help us! Lord, help us!*

I had no clue as to the massiveness of the situation we were facing, nor was I prepared. When I walked into the waiting room, I saw Tony's mom sitting there, bathed with tears flowing down her face. She'd learned about the tragedy and rushed to the hospital. Oh my gosh, I will never forget the pain that exuded through her. We held each other and cried out of control. As the spouse, I had to be the one to see him, to identify him, and I was beyond devastated. The pain, the hurt, the agony is something we will never forget. I still don't understand why this had to happen. That was the worst day of my life.

After Burger drove me home from the hospital, he said, "I need about three to four hours to get in touch with some people in the fire department and the fire chief to see how all this will play out. I want you to think about what you want to do, funeral wise. If you have a church in mind…I know you're not in the right place to do this, but think about it."

He was right. I wasn't in the right place, nor the right emotional or physical state to bury my husband. Who would be? To this day, I thank God for John Burger and John Faulkner, who was Burger's "sidekick."

Hayden met me at the door and embraced me tightly as he wept. He and his brother-in-law had a remarkably close and loving relationship. I was functioning in a state of confusion. I wasn't sure how I was feeling or why any of this had happened. The loss overwhelmed my heart with pain. How was I going to tell our children they would not see their daddy anymore? Struggling to contain myself, I told my brother, "I must tell the boys, and I must tell them now."

How does a mother tell her young children that their daddy wasn't coming home, and they will never see him again? I envisioned having many talks with my sons about many life-enhancing and altering topics, but no one prepared me for this one. In retrospect, I don't think anyone could have. As an adult, death itself is difficult to comprehend, let alone for a child. However, someone had to do it, and I was now the head of the house. I had to learn how to wear two hats, how to cope without my husband, and this conversation was my starting point.

I took a few deep breaths and called both boys into the kitchen. I sat them on my lap, enfolding them in my arms. I cuddled them as I tried to find the right words while fighting to hold back the tears.

I said to Lil' Tony, "Do you remember when Mother Pool went home to be with the Lord?" Mother Pool was an elder in the church who babysat him and passed away before his dad.

Lil' Tony replied, "Yes."

"Your daddy went home to be with the Lord."

He looked up at me, his little eyes filling up with tears. "Mommy, I wish God could have given my daddy another chance."

From his lips to my ears, I felt as if my heart shattered into shards. I held him and Arzel, as we cried. Arzel, at the tender age of twenty-one months, couldn't comprehend what was happening. There are moments in life you never forget. That moment I will remember and cherish forever.

I've often heard people refer to a child as being an "old soul." Lil' Tony was an old soul. Much like his dad, he has a calm spirit. After a while, he jumped down from my lap and went downstairs to where he and his dad would play their Sony PlayStation games, and his brother followed.

A minute later, Lil' Tony returned, climbed in my lap, and looked me in the eyes. "Mommy, are you okay?"

"Yes."

"Okay," he said, climbing down from my lap and went to check on his brother.

I didn't know what to do or how to feel. I was numb. I went to my boys, held them, and cried.

Again, Arzel was only twenty-one months old, so there was no way he would have been able to understand what I'd shared with his brother moments earlier. He had no idea what was going on. The thought of our children growing up without their dad and how it would affect them ran rampant through my head. Also, Arzel being so young, the thought of him never remembering his dad was so painful for me to accept.

For the rest of that morning, I functioned in a daze. Yet, drained and overwhelmed with emotions, I welcomed the outpour of telephone calls and people visiting our home to extend their condolences and offering their help. I was truly surprised by how many people were already aware of what occurred. I didn't realize that even before I learned of the tragedy, the media was already covering the story about the deadly "Fire on Cherry Road" and the first firefighter to die on the scene, Anthony "Sauce" Phillips from Engine 10. This was much more than what I understood it to be. It was much more than Tony perishing in the "line of duty." The extent of the tragedy was beyond belief and included another line of duty death and extensive injuries to other firefighters. *None of this seemed real!*

CHAPTER Five

The Fire on Cherry Road, NE

When I decided to write this book, I knew I would have to include details regarding the fire on Cherry Road, NE. In order to recount the night my husband died in the line of duty, or as much of it as possible, I interviewed Tony's fellow firefighters and extensively read writings and reports on this topic, much of which you will read in this chapter. Although twenty years later, I still find it overwhelming and emotional, getting choked up when I discuss Tony with his fellow coworkers, reminiscing on a painful part of the past. The pain of the loss has never left me.

I must preface that although it is public knowledge, I chose to omit the address on Cherry Road, NE for the privacy of the current owner. This also includes his first name.

In his 2002 thesis, "Does Fire Culture Influence Firefighter Death and Injury?", Edward M. Pearson, former DC Deputy Fire Chief, probed the relationship between the fire service culture, fireground death, and injury. He stated, "The fire service culture is one that embraces its own after they have "proven" themselves; accepts praises from the public; sets their own standards for bravery; and, does not condone cowardliness. Actions that many consider unsafe and potentially deadly, the fire service culture considers it an honor to perform and the passageway into this elite profession."

As of 2015, there were 1,160,450 professional firefighters in the United States.[3] I'm sure, at the publication of this book, many more heroic persons have joined the ranks. Firefighters fight active fires or make emergency medical calls as a result of illnesses, accidental injuries, or disasters. Firefighters, like Anthony "Sauce" Phillips, save lives and millions of dollars a year in property damage.

The firefighters of Engine Company 10 in northeast Washington, DC, are among the firefighters who fight fires and saves lives, as it is one of the busiest stations in the United States, responding to an average of seven thousand calls per year, from burning buildings to medical emergencies to people who need a ride to the hospital. With an arduous pace, and located in the Trinidad and Fort Lincoln neighborhoods, it is one of the most sought-after assignments in the city's fire and EMS department. It is the station where every firefighter wants to work, and this was no different for Tony.

The Memorial holiday weekend was not unusual from any other. Engine 10 continued to live up to its reputation as the busiest engine company in Washington, DC, let alone

---

[3] "The U.S. Fire Department Profile through 2015 Fact Sheet," National Fire Protection Agency, Research, Data & Analytics, 2015, www.nfpa.org.

the nation. However, little did we know, this weekend would go down in history.

Early on May 30 at seventeen minutes past midnight, the 911 Communications Center received a telephone call reporting a fire at a property on Cherry Road, NE.

Cherry Road, NE is nestled in the Fort Lincoln area of northeast DC and is a development of townhomes. This particular townhome is a two-story with a basement, three bedrooms, two and one-half baths, and approximately one thousand eight hundred eighty-one square feet. From the front exterior, it looks like a two-story home. However, the rear exterior shows the basement level. Upon entering the front door, to the right is a staircase leading up to the upper level with the bedrooms. To the left is the kitchen. Ahead is a small hallway leading to the combined living room and dining room space. At the entrance to this combined space, to the right is a door that opens to the staircase that leads down into the basement. The basement is where the fire started.

The residents of the property, Ezra and Laverne Naughton, who had lived there for ten years, were stirred from sleep by the smoke alarm. Mrs. Naughton went downstairs to the first floor and found smoke and heat. Wisely, they left the house through the front door, leaving it open.

"During the day, we had done some gardening work in our front patio area," recounted Mrs. Naughton, who was very gracious to sit down with me to talk about her experience and the fire. "It was a beautiful day and we were outside planting flowers. That night, I recall that the windows were up in the house. Just a beautiful breezy night. We went to bed about eleven o'clock. I woke up and smelled smoke. It was coming through the vents, but I thought it was coming through the windows because they were up. My husband, who was twenty-five years older than me, was sleeping. So, I jumped up and ran downstairs. When you go down the stairs, you go straight to the front door. I made a right turn and a wall of heat just hit me. I realized I'd better not go any further.

"I ran back upstairs to grab him. Nobody had on any clothes, so we ran downstairs to the hall closet. I grabbed a coat and ran out the front door first and banged on neighbors' doors. Meanwhile, he was still at the front entrance, in the closet, getting a coat. I yelled to him, telling him he had to hurry up and get out of the house.

"At that point, we were standing out on the sidewalk. Our ADT system had gone off. I remember going into a neighbor's house—we had to run around to the rear—and I saw the firetrucks coming from the rear. I yelled out to them, 'Everybody is out! Everybody is out!'"

Communications dispatched four engines and two truck companies, a battalion fire chief, and a rescue squad. Less than two minutes later, a second 911 call provided a corrected address of the property on Cherry Road, NE, reporting a fire in the basement.

Communications passed on the change of address, although only one of the responding fire companies acknowledged it. However, Engines 10 and 26 were the first engines on the scene within four minutes of dispatch, and at approximately 00:24:00, firefighters entered the first floor via the front door, to which they were met by thick, billowing smoke and extreme heat. Among the firefighters from Engines 10 and 26 were Tony and Louis Matthews.

According to many reports I've read, within two minutes, firefighters took out the front window on the first floor to provide additional ventilation. Removal of the window was from the inside due to obstructions from security bars on the outside. Firefighters also opened windows on the second story at the front of the house.

Another fire team positioned by sliding glass doors on the basement level reported that the basement was full of smoke, but there seemed to be very little fire. Despite significant confusion over the exact location of the firefighters upstairs, a decision was made to break out the basement's sliding glass doors. At this time, Tony had entered the home from the front entrance on the first floor.

It is my understanding that there were several small fires on the floor of the basement that rapidly increased in size after breaking the sliding glass doors. Yet, despite my understanding, after speaking with an unnamed source, I learned that at the back of the house, the fire hose was too short to reach the door. That hose was left unattended while the firefighter secured a longer hose from the firetruck. During that time, another firefighter approached the back, saw the unattended hose on the ground, picked it up, aimed at the glass patio doors, and released the powerful stream of water, breaking the glass. At that exact moment, Tony was on the first level, opening the door to the basement. An intense surge of heat rushed up the staircase and through the door, killing Tony. "The coroner said it microwaved him," said the unnamed source. Thus, came the first report of a firefighter down. It was Tony.

The Fire on Cherry Road, NE

As the fire quickly intensified, the firefighters received orders to vacate the basement before it became engulfed in a full-fledged inferno.

When I learned of the fire, so many thoughts went through my head, but I couldn't stop asking one question: "Did he suffer?"

Almost twenty years later, while working on this book, I asked this question to John Burger, who later become a dear friend.

"I don't think he suffered," he said. "I think because of the blast of heat he got hit with, his lungs were seared. He wasn't lying there in agony for a long period of time. Probably ten seconds."

While it was good to hear John say he didn't think Tony suffered, as I think back to that day, and twenty years without my husband, I'm still suffering. With life, you can do two things: standstill and allow it to pass you by or move along with it. If for no other reason, I moved along with life for the sake of my two sons, who, going forward, would only get to know their father through stories told by me, family, friends, and fellow firefighters.

From what I've learned, paramedics worked on Tony from the moment they left Cherry Road until they arrived at Washington Hospital Center. Tony was pronounced dead twenty-three minutes upon arrival, becoming the 96th firefighter to die in the line of duty. Firefighter Louis Matthews (Engine Company 26), the 97th, died the following day because of his injuries, the first double line-of-duty deaths in almost ninety years for Washington, DC's fire service.

Two other firefighters sustained minor injuries, but a third, Fire Sergeant Joe Morgan, also from Engine Company 26, spent approximately one hundred eighty days in the hospital and underwent multiple surgical procedures for burns, moving him into retirement.

It was the very routine nature of the fire and its tragic outcome that prompted the District of Columbia Fire and Emergency Medical Services Department Reconstruction Committee to request a full investigation into the fire dynamics of the incident, of which I call a "tragedy." The loss of anyone, whether in the line of duty, from illness, or due to natural causes is a tragedy.

Investigators determined the fire started near an electrical fixture in the ceiling of the basement and that the actual fire may have taken several hours to develop to a flaming stage. As the fire spread from the ignition source, first along the ceiling and then to other items in the basement, it first developed quickly but then depleted the supply of oxygen necessary for combustion.

However, it was the breaking open of the basement door that created the firestorm, providing outside air into a pre-heated but under-ventilated fire compartment, which then developed into a post-flashover fire within sixteen seconds. In other words, putting it in layman terms, breaking the sliding glass doors allowed in oxygen (e.g., air), so when Tony opened the basement door from the first floor, fire gushed up the stairwell with a high velocity at, what was reported, approximately eighteen miles per hour, like a speeding inferno. Tony didn't have a chance.

The Cherry Road fire changed the lives of so many people. The fire destroyed all the Naughton's belongings, precious artifacts, photographs, and memories. After living months in a hotel room, their home was renovated. Yet, it didn't feel the same for them. Eventually, they sold their home. It took the life of my husband and sons' father. It took the life of another young firefighter. It caused severe burn injuries to another firefighter, leaving him unable to continue to fulfill his duties. It left life-long emotional and internal hurt to the men and women who heroically perform this difficult job. It's been twenty years, and though we've moved on with life, and so has Mrs. Naughton (at the writing of this book, Mr. Naughton had passed), the memory of that night will live with us forever.

After the fire, Cherry Road became an attraction of love, as friends, strangers, and loved ones of Tony and Louis Matthews laid flowers, cards of sympathy, and adorable stuffed animals at the front door and along the sidewalk. On the back wooden gate of the property, "RIP AP" was prominently spray painted.

One summer afternoon in 2018, after visiting Tony's grave at Fort Lincoln Cemetery, I contemplated whether I should stop by the property, as I had never visited the site, not once. But because I chose to write this story about the loss of my husband at the Cherry Road fire and how it impacted family, friends and firefighters, I thought it would be the right time to meet the owners. I wasn't sure what to expect. I drove to the location, which was about three minutes away. I pulled into a parking space in the community and sat in my vehicle for about five minutes, trying to build up the nerve to knock on the front door. It was exceedingly difficult, and I was nervous, but I stood at the front door and rang the doorbell. To my surprise, a gentleman opened the door. I was expecting Mr. or Mrs. Naughton.

In a trembling, soft voice, I said, "Hello, my name is Lysa Phillips, the widow of the late Firefighter Anthony Phillips."

Before I could give him more information, he introduced himself as Mr. Smith and the current owner of the home. "I know who you are," he said.

I stood in front of his door with a distressed, internal feeling. My heartbeat felt like it was slowing.

Mr. Smith invited me in.

"That's okay," I said, with hesitancy. I was in such a disconcerted state; I didn't know how to respond. I wasn't sure if he sensed my anxiety.

"It's okay," he uttered sympathetically.

I stepped inside and stood at the entrance for a few seconds, trying to keep my composure. I felt Tony's spirit at once. It was a very calming feeling. I began to visualize what occurred as if I was present on that dreadful night of May 30.

As we walked down the hallway, Mr. Smith said he had purchased the home in August 2000. Standing only a few feet away from the same spot my husband lost his life, to say I was overwhelmed with emotions would be an understatement. I told him I was writing the book and wanted to get a visual of the inside of the home to understand how this tragedy resulted in such major losses and injuries. It surprised me to see that the house was smaller than I had expected.

Mr. Smith and I talked for about an hour. I asked him if I could come back to talk more in-depth and take photos of his home to insert in the book. He agreed.

"I look forward to reading it," he replied.

I sat in my vehicle for a little while to digest what had just happened. I finally had an opportunity to visit the home after all these years.

A few weeks later, I went back to see Mr. Smith. I learned that prior to acquiring the property, he was not aware of the fire that transpired in the very place he called home. "It wasn't until a memorial that took place at the park directly across from here," said Mr. Smith when asked how he felt after he learned about the tragedy, "that it really cemented in my head what had occurred, and it prompted me to look on the government's website and I saw the reenactment. When the firemen congregated at the park, and you [Lysa] was out there as well, I was taken aback. Because I didn't want to live in a mausoleum. And that's what I felt like. I felt a little uncomfortable being here. Friends of mine told me that what happened here created a path for me to be where I am, and that I had to look at it as a blessing and not that I had a fault in what happened."

Mr. Smith took me on a tour around his beautiful home. The layout was the same as it was prior to the fire. As I walked through the rooms on the first level, I painted pictures in my mind of how they looked after the fire and could imagine the torture my husband and the other firefighters might have endured. Pain pierced through my heart as I relived those terrifying moments when I learned that my husband lost his life in the line of duty.

I stood silently in front of the closed door, leading to the basement, in the spot where Tony's motionless body laid on that dreadful night. I took a few deep breaths. I was struggling to control my emotions as the thought of how the "flashover" occurred and caused the death of my loving husband when he opened that door. Nothing could have prepared him or his fellow firefighters for this. How could this have happened? How?

I built up the courage to open the door, with Mr. Smith following closely. We talked as we walked down the stairs. I tried to focus on our conversations to avoid trying to figure out what could have really gone wrong. We toured the basement and the back-patio area. Mr. Smith showed me the location where the electrical fire started and the sliding glass doors to the back patio that the firefighters had broken. It surprised me to see that the residue of the intense smoke was still on the brick patio walls.

With Mr. Smith's permission, I took several photos of the inside and outside of the house.

Taken from the front door, in the foyer. Steps to the right, hallway leading to the living and dining room areas. The kitchen to the left.

The Fire on Cherry Road, NE

This is the door leading to the basement. This is the spot where my husband lost his life.

The beautiful living room.

The stairs leading to and from the basement.

Basement interior from the outside.

The Fire on Cherry Road, NE

Rear of the townouse, basement level.

Back patio. Twenty years of smoke is still evident on the wall.

Despite the loss of our loved one, and I can only speak for me, Tony's death was not in vain. The fire resulted in major changes in firefighting policies, procedures, and training.

According to a report published by the UL Firefighter Safety Research Institute (FSRI), ...*below grade fires can present different challenges based on the potential ventilation or the building construction. ... field experience was collected and reviewed, and fire experiments were conducted as part of a collaborative effort between the FSRI and the International Society of Fire Service Instructors (ISFSI) to increase the effectiveness of fighting a basement fire and to reduce the high risk to firefighters through the "Understanding and Fighting Basement Fires" research project. The incident on Cherry Road was a catalyst to better understand fire dynamics in structures, a mission that continues today.*[4]

According to *DC Watch*[5], Fire Chief Donald Edwards (now retired) appointed a Reconstruction Committee to investigate and evaluate the emergency response activities at this fire. This report is the result of extensive interviews, independent investigation, and evaluation of the reports of other investigators. The Reconstruction Committee has found that the District of Columbia Fire and EMS Department (Department) has several deficiencies, particularly in training, staffing. equipment, and administration. The mere knowledge of these shortcomings and recommended actions does

---

[4]https://ulfirefightersafety.org/research-projects/understanding-and-fighting-basement-fires.html

[5](http://www.dcwatch.com/govern/fire000530.htm)

nothing. Many of the recommendations contained in this report are the same recommendations made in a report of the investigation of the death of Sergeant John Carter in the Kennedy Street fire of October 24, 1997. Further inaction on these recommendations cannot be tolerated.

The Reconstruction Committee determined that the deficiencies in operations and equipment resulting in these deaths fall into the following categories.

- Firefighter accountability (e.g., company officers failed to keep personnel together and operate as a team; personnel did not use the "Mayday" alert when firefighters were discovered missing)

- Fireground command (e.g., the Incident Commander failed to establish a fixed command post; did not have an aide and was thus unable to coordinate front and rear teams; failed to sector the incident)

- Communications (e.g., no size-up report of the rear was provided; interior companies did not make radio transmissions of their initial attack and progress; it was impossible for injured firefighters to communicate information because they did not have radios)

- Company/unit operations (e.g., actions of companies were not coordinated, so the actions of some companies threatened the safety of others; some officers and firefighters worked alone or with other companies instead of staying with their own companies; truck companies were inadequately staffed)

- Safety (e.g., PASS (Personal Alert Safety Systems) devices that help locate firefighters who are immobile were not in use by each firefighter; the Department's Safety Office lacks the staffing and authority to conduct appropriate investigations and follow-up on safety recommendations)

- Administration (e.g., nearly identical recommendations, made following the Kennedy Street fire were not acted upon, resulting in many of the same problems at this incident; personnel do not receive adequate training in live fires because the Department's fire training building is unusable)

Prayerfully, these changes will be effective and will avoid such occurrences in the future, preventing families from having to experience the hurt and pain our families have had to bear from losing our loved one in the line of duty.

Every year, Engine Company 10 takes probationary firefighters to the Cherry Road property. Representatives from the Fire Training Academy would also bring the new recruits to view the site.

"On the recent visit," Mr. Smith continued. "I wanted to invite them inside, but I was working. I know the visits are designed to educate and train the new recruits, and I thought if they could see the inside it would give them a visual of the layout of the house."

As I expressed my gratitude to Mr. Smith for allowing me to visit his home and speak with him, the spirit of the Lord wanted me to leave him with some words of comfort. I spoke as the Lord led me. "I believe Tony took his last breath right here, and the spirit you say you feel is his spirit. Just know that it will always be present in your home to comfort you."

"I definitely felt it," he responded passionately.

Note: Adapted from *Report from the Reconstruction Committee: Fire at ▮ Cherry Road NE, Washington DC, May 30, 1999*, p. 17. District of Columbia Fire & EMS, 2000 and *Simulation of Dynamics of the Fire at ▮ Cherry Road NE, Washington D.C., May 30, 1999*, p. 5, by Daniel Madrzykowski & Robert Vettori, 2000. Gaithersburg, MD: National Institute of Standards and Technology.

He Answered the Call

Note: Adapted from *Report from the Reconstruction Committee: Fire at ▬ Cherry Road NE, Washington DC, May 30, 1999*, p. 19. District of Columbia Fire & EMS, 2000 and *Simulation of the Dynamics of the Fire at ▬ Cherry Road NE, Washington D.C., May 30, 1999*, p. 5, by Daniel Madrzykowski & Robert Vettori, 2000. Gaithersburg, MD: National Institute of Standards and Technology.

Conditions on Side A at Aproximately 00:28

Note: From *Report from the Reconstruction Committee: Fire at ▪▪▪ Cherry Road NE, Washington DC, May 30, 1999*, p. 29. District of Columbia Fire & EMS, 2000.

Post-Fire Conditions on Floor 1

Note: Adapted from *Report from the Reconstruction Committee: Fire at ▪▪▪ Cherry Road NE, Washington DC, May 30, 1999*, p. 20. District of Columbia Fire & EMS, 2000.

Conditions on Side C at Aproximately 00:28

Note: From *Report from the Reconstruction Committee: Fire at*  *Cherry Road NE, Washington DC, May 30, 1999*, p. 32. District of Columbia Fire & EMS, 2000.

The Fire on Cherry Road, NE

Note: Adapted from *Report from the Reconstruction Committee: Fire at ███ Cherry Road NE, Washington DC, May 30, 1999*, p. 18 & 20. District of Columbia Fire & EMS, 2000; *Simulation of the Dynamics of the Fire at ███ Cherry Road NE, Washington D.C., May 30, 1999*, p. 12-13, by Daniel Madrzykowski & Robert Vettori, 2000. Gaithersburg, MD: National Institute of Standards and Technology, and NIOSH Death in the Line of Duty Report 99 F-21, 1999, p. 19.

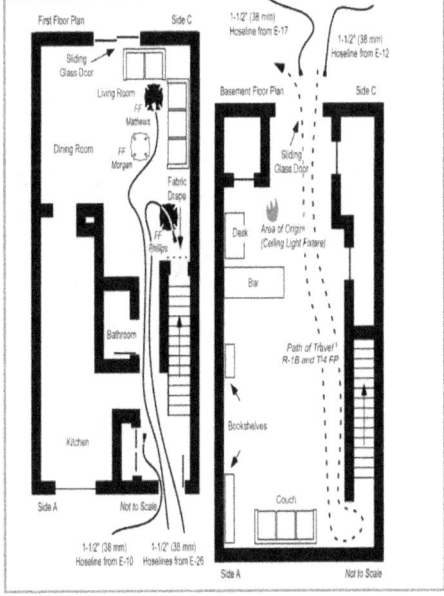

He Answered the Call

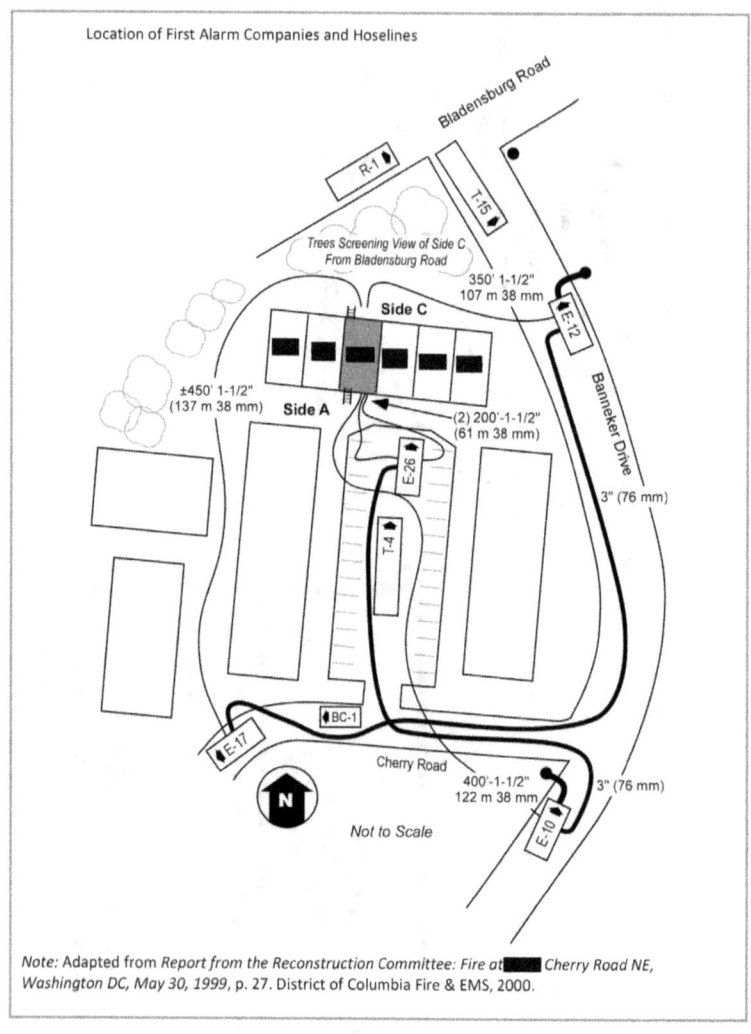

Note: Adapted from *Report from the Reconstruction Committee: Fire at ▮▮▮ Cherry Road NE, Washington DC, May 30, 1999*, p. 27. District of Columbia Fire & EMS, 2000.

CHAPTER Six

Our Dad, the Hero

Throughout life, one expects to suffer a traumatic experience or two. In most instances, those experiences help mold us into resilient, humble adults. The loss of a parent is one of those tragic expectations, as it is a part of life's cycle. However, for two young boys, the loss of a parent—a father—was a tragedy they should have never had to experience until they had become grown men.

Six-year-old Anthony, Jr. and twenty-one-month-old Arzel Phillips experienced the loss of their dad. A loss no child should have to experience at such a young age.

That dreadful morning of May 30, when I returned from the hospital and had to share with our boys that their dad had perished and went home to be with the Lord, was the worst and most painful thing I could have ever shared with

He Answered the Call

Lil' Tony and Arzel.

them. Understanding the close and loving relationship they had with their dad, I knew revealing the devastating news would shatter their tender, young hearts—which it did. I wish this wasn't something I had to do. I wish my husband and the father of our children didn't work that night; then, we wouldn't have to hurt and mourn for him…and I wouldn't be writing this book.

Sitting my children on my lap to share the shocking news with them, particularly Lil' Tony, as he was the oldest and could comprehend life and death to a certain extent, I did not know what type of reaction I would receive from them other than tears. Yes, there were tears and emotional reactions and wishing God would have given their daddy another chance; but to my amazement, they showed tremendous, loving concern for me. As we hugged and cried, I was in awe of how they made such an effort to console me, as Lil' Tony asked me repeatedly, "Mom, are you okay?"

I learned a lot from my boys on that day. Their strength was beyond what I could have ever imagined. It brings me back to the days when their dad would leave. He would always tell Lil' Tony, "When I'm not here, I need you to make sure you lock the doors, turn on the alarm, and take care of Mommy and Arzel." He always followed his dad's instructions.

But after his dad passed, he took on and carried out his duties to another level. Lil' Tony felt that he was now the man of the house, and it was obvious to the people who came to visit us and offered help to the family. I recall, in a house filled with people, Lil' Tony stood at the top of the stairs of our home and demanded everyone's attention…

"Hello, everyone! Hello, everyone!" he yelled out in a profoundly serious tone. "I am no longer Lil' Tony. Call me Tony!"

People looked upon him in amazement. They were surprised and impressed to see this six-year-old boy take on the role of the head of the household. He stepped into his daddy's shoes. But he was only doing what his dad had instructed him to do in his absence. Of course, no one, including me, expected him to assume such a huge responsibility at six.

Raising two young children, who were going through the pain of the sudden loss of their father, was not easy, nor was it easy for them to grasp. Daddy had always been there, and now he was no longer around. I saw the emotional and mental distress both my sons endured, day-by-day. Consoling them and helping them to cope was not easy. Although they were strong in some ways, the effect it had on them was nothing I would want to see any child experience. I kept them in the church as normal and tried to keep them active in sports activities and focused on other things to redirect their minds and thoughts. Their dad's fellow firefighters from Engine 10 included them in various outings, such as hockey, basketball, and baseball games.

Several weeks after Tony passed, one of the most profound situations occurred on a Sunday on our way to church. As the boys and I talked about their dad, Lil' Tony said to me, "Ma, on May 1st, God told me that my daddy was going to die."

That stunned me. My immediate response was, "Why didn't you tell me?"

"Because I didn't want to hurt you."

Lil' Tony at outing with firefighters and children after dad's death.

Arzel playing with a member of the Washington Wizards.

I could not believe my six-year-old baby spoke such mature words.

We rode the rest of the way to church, but because my mind was at unrest, I could not stay for the entire service. I tried my best to dissect what I had heard from my son. Thinking more on what he said brought me back to May 1.

A church member wrote a play, in which Tony and I were the main characters. On May 1, our church performed the play at a school in DC. Following the play, a Spirit-filled minister prophesied that there would be a "shakening" up at the church. No one knew what the "shakening" up would be. Low and behold, Tony died at the end of the month. Since Tony was such an instrumental person in the church he grew up in, I believe this prophecy was a reference to Tony going home to be with the Lord. Therefore, God prepared Lil' Tony for his daddy's death and what he would go through. I think knowing his dad would be gone gave Lil' Tony the ability to handle the loss in such a peaceful way, as well as giving him the strength to console his brother and me.

As the years passed and the boys were on the path to becoming young men, I felt that not having their dad to teach them the fundamentals of manhood would have a significant impact on their growth. I believe every male child needs a real man [dad] to give them guidance as they mature into an adult. Well, my boys didn't have their dad to guide them. As their mother, I was only able to make sure they understood that God is the foundation of their lives, they received a good education, and teach them values, morals, and respect and how to love and care for themselves and others. I was not able to teach them the physical and masculine things a father could instill in them. Nevertheless, I didn't have any problems with them. They have always been wonderful children who took care of each other—big brother, little brother. Among other things, I have always been proud of their close relationship.

However, even with a Godly upbringing, losing their dad weighed heavy on their hearts. Lil' Tony was older, had more time with his dad, and remembers more, but Arzel's recollection is vague. He has faint memories of his interaction with his father, though photos have helped to define some of them, leading him to remember more. There were periods of dark times when he'd expressed his pain of not having his dad around. I have had to comfort him on those occasions with encouragement and prayer. Both of my sons have expressed wanting to hear his voice, wanting to know what he sounded like, and learning what they both have in common with him. It's amazing the similarities and characteristics they both share with their dad.

Twenty years later...Arzel (twenty-one), Tony (twenty-six).

"I remember I was in my mom's bed," began Lil' Tony, who is now twenty-six years old, when asked about the day he learned his dad wasn't coming home. "I think my grandma and uncle were in the other room, and my mom was crying. The house was full of people and it confused me. I came down the steps and saw my mom crying. I asked her what was wrong, and she told me. Everything else is fuzzy.

"My mom told me what happened. She said he went to see Jesus. At that age, I couldn't comprehend death. It saddened me, but it didn't hit me until I got older. Now, when I look back at the videos of the day of the funeral, I see a little kid walking into the church, chilling as if nothing was going on. That's where I was then."

Through his growing years, Lil' Tony compartmentalized the loss of his dad. Not that he didn't want to deal with it, he just didn't know how. Now that he is an adult, he talks about what it was like growing up without his dad.

"A big chunk of my preteen and teenage years, I didn't deal with it. Since my mom remarried, my stepfather played the role of the father during that time. So, I didn't feel like I'd lost out on having a father. But when he and my mom divorced, that feeling of not having a father returned. I unpacked what I had compartmentalized and tried to deal with it.

"When I worked at Providence Hospital, I came in contact with many firefighters who either knew or have heard of my dad. Those who knew him told me stories about him, which was nice. They also told me about "that day." They spoke highly of him. Talking to them made me feel like, yeah, he was real. They filled that void for me. Now I know a lot of traits I get from my mom because I can see it, but the other traits I know come from my dad."

"There have been times when I wished I had my dad to help me through, to give me advice, and so on. I feel a connection with my father. He died very heroically, and I'm proud of him. He died doing what he loved."

I have always hoped that the children would not have an interest in following in their dad's footsteps in becoming a firefighter. I have tried not to have such conversations with them regarding that line of work. However, now that they are adults—twenty-six and twenty-one—Lil' Tony has decided to pursue the profession. Of our two sons, I have always known that if either of them would have an interest, it would be Tony, Jr. He has the distinctive qualities it takes to do this kind of work. Plus, he received his degree in exercise science and worked in physical therapy, which is a segue into the occupation. Also, while working in outpatient rehabilitation at the hospital, he treated many of his dad's fellow brothers and sisters from the fire department. I knew, as they recognized him as Sauce's son when they met him, they would try to encourage him to follow in his dad's footsteps. Yet, he was adamant about letting his dad's legacy live on and did not express an interest in becoming a firefighter.

Over time, with great thought and consideration, Tony decided he wanted to pursue a career in this field and join the men and women whose purpose is to protect people and places, rescue people from burning structures and other treacherous situations, and provide emergency medical care at the site of incidents—these and more of the duties of a firefighter—just as his dad did.

Arzel, on the other hand, has more of the creative qualities and does not have interest in the firefighting world currently.

"I don't remember anything about the day my dad passed. I have certain images, but that's about it. Was I able to comprehend what was going on? No. I think around the age of four or five is when it was really explained to me, but even still I couldn't comprehend it. Though, it is still being explained to me to this day.

"I don't know if I miss him, because you can't really miss someone you don't remember. I think I've coped with not having my dad around, up to this point. Now that I'm older, circumstances will change, and I'm sure I'll need that fatherly guidance. I'm sure things would be different in my life if he was here.

"My brother, Tony, is like a father to me, even if he doesn't know or see it. I follow his footsteps. Like Tony, I've heard stories about my dad from people who knew him, and I believe my dad was one amazing man."

Arzel is in college, majoring in communications, and doing what he enjoys—photography and videography. His focus is on a career in that direction. Arzel has always been the one who expresses most of his hurt and emotions of not having his dad to father him and teach him the things a father instructs his son. However, the hurt and pain did not distract him nor his brother from becoming respectful men with hearts of gold.

Tony and Arzel will always identify their dad as a hero and as a firefighter who placed his life on the line to save others as Christ did for His children.

"Our dad, Anthony Sean "Sauce" Phillips, the hero, lives!"

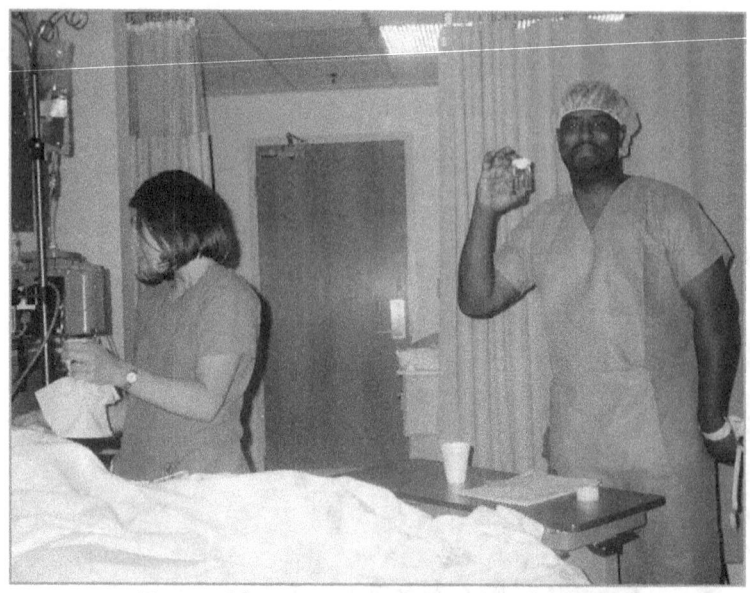

Tony in delivery room, waiting on Arzel's arrival.

Celebrating Arzel's 1st birthday.

Our Dad, the Hero

He Answered the Call

Big Tony and Lil' Tony.

Our Dad, the Hero

The U.S. flag presented to the family.

Me and the boys after Tony died.

Lil' Tony, Arzel, and me with the Washington Wizards.

Our Dad, the Hero

Tony, Jr.

He Answered the Call

Arzel

CHAPTER Seven

The Difference He Made in Our Lives

Family, friends, and co-workers are exceptionally significant in our lives. They are there to support and comfort us in times of sadness and to rejoice with us during good times. They make themselves available to help carry us through when our burdens get so heavy and difficult to bear. Tony did just that. He was always there to help lighten our load when things got a bit tough, gave profound advice when necessary, made us laugh, and celebrated with us.

When I surrendered to God's demand to compose this book, I didn't want it to be a story from my view only. I wanted to include a few individuals that the tragedy affected personally, including family, friends, and firefighters who were present on that day or worked with Tony directly. Therefore, I interviewed a select few to get their narrative about their personal and professional relationship with Tony and how the loss had an impact on their lives during that time and over these twenty years. There were several immediate family members who could not share their story due to the tremendous pain and suffering they are enduring to this day.

I knew discussing this tragedy with the persons who shared their thoughts and feelings in this book would be painful, as it was for me; however, without their input, I didn't think I would be able to deliver the story's objective as it relates to "coping and healing" appropriately. Interviewing each person was emotional, as they reached back to that time of pain and sorrow. We shared tears and prayed together. This opportunity allowed me to capture what Tony meant to many.

As they cope, amazingly, after all these years, several of them have not dealt fully with their pain of losing Tony. Some have expressed anger. Some have expressed disappointment. Some have expressed disbelief. Some have questioned what occurred. But all have expressed the good times they'd experienced with him. With their permission, the stories shared in this book are their testaments from their perspectives. Some will make you smile. Some may make you cry. Tony meant a lot to many, and they treasured their relationship with him. For that reason, their personal story or account of what happened that terrible night on May 30, 1999, needed to be told in their own words.

I could have had a substantial number of Tony's friends and family members to share their love for him in words in this book, but I know the book wouldn't have an end. He was a devoted friend to many, which was indisputable when he lived as well as when he died, as witnessed by the outpour of people who came out to pay respect to this gracious man of God who lived to fulfill his Heavenly Father's purpose.

"I had known Tony for almost four years. We attended the same church. But I actually came to find out that I knew him from high school. We both attended Theodore Roosevelt in the District. Tony and I were very cool, like brother and sister. He was that guy that Lysa could trust to hang out with me and others and was okay with it. We were all friends, more like family. When I became part of his, Lysa's, and Lil' Tony's lives, we spent a lot of time together at their home, in church, and hanging out. I was one of Lysa's best friends in the play we performed on May 1.

"When Lysa got pregnant with Arzel, they insisted I, along with another close friend, GeGe, be co-godmothers of Arzel. I didn't hesitate to say 'Yes.'"

LaTonya has always been a dedicated friend; one you could depend on in any circumstance. She was one of the

LaTonya holding Arzel, her godson.

first persons to be present at the hospital on the day of Arzel's birth. She didn't leave my side, sleeping on the floor in front of my hospital room at times, waiting for him to come and being available if I needed something.

"You could only imagine how I felt when I received that phone call of Tony's death that morning from another member of the church, whose son was also a firefighter. It was surreal. I sat up in bed in disbelief, trying to figure out if it was real. I was numb for the first few hours. But we were instructed by our pastor not to visit Lysa. Because of our close relationship, I called her to see if she needed anything. I wanted to be there for her and the boys, so I asked, 'Is it okay for me to come over?' Without hesitation, she said, 'Yes.'

"People were in and out of the house throughout the day. All-hands-on-deck, whatever they needed, the church family was there. For about two weeks, I was by Lysa's side to make sure things were done in the house and to help look after the boys as she took care of business. It was difficult trying to stay strong for the family, but I had to for Lysa. But then, when I went home and I had my chance to release my pain, I cried and cried and cried.

"Today, I have a deeper respect for firefighters. And sometimes, when I hear about the death of a firefighter, I always go back to that day. I go past the street where he died at least once or twice a week because I live in that area, but my memories are good memories. I am not sad anymore; I've gotten through that part. When I see the firetrucks go by, I always send up a prayer, asking God to cover them and put a wedge of protection over them.

"I loved how he loved his sons. I know he didn't have many years with Arzel, but just witnessing his connection with those boys, no one could ever deny his love for them. But that was only a reflection of the way he was raised with love. Oh my gosh, he loved his mother, and she loved him, without a doubt.

"Family extended beyond his immediate family. You knew things would be okay when Tony was around, whether in the church or anywhere else. So, when you had him as a friend, you had a real friend, somebody you could talk to and would give you anything you needed if he had it to give. If he didn't have it, he'd get it and you had it. That was Tony! I have heard the saying, 'You can remember what somebody said, but you will never forget how they made you feel.' He always saw the good in people and always had a positive impact on the lives of people he met. I was once in sorrow, but I am no longer, because my friend and brother in Christ is a hero and he went out in a hero's fashion."

—*LaTonya Robinson, Family Friend and Former Member of Bethesda New Life Gospel Church*

"Tony and I had a good relationship that was built around him being my sister's boyfriend then husband. As their relationship flourished, our relationship grew also, and I respected him more. When he became a father and I saw the way he changed his life, I had even more respect for him.

"When Lysa called the house to let the family know what happened, my initial reaction was 'No way!' I instantly hopped in my vehicle and went to Lysa and Tony's house. As I was driving over there, I still couldn't grasp what was going on. Being there for my sister and nephews was a no-brainer. Lysa and I have a close relationship. Whenever she needs me, I'm there for her, and she needed me.

"Losing Tony impacted my life more so because Lysa wasn't happy, my nephews lost their father, and I lost a good friend. The boys would have to grow up without their dad and that hurt my feelings. Tony Jr. only knew him for a little while and Arzel wouldn't have the chance to know him, which was upsetting. I got to know Tony on different levels, but his sons never got that opportunity.

"I believe my sister's strength during her loss comes from our mom. Throughout her life, she witnessed how my mom would handle difficult situations and persevere. Lysa learned how to deal with difficult situations from the best."

— *Hayden Lambert, Brother of Lysa Phillips*

"Tony was an incredible young man, whom we loved dearly. We were in Richmond when I heard about his death. I just happened to call Pam McFadden, who now has transitioned. I can't remember what I was calling Pam for, but she said, 'Carolyn, have you heard?'

"I said, 'What, Pam?'

"She said, 'Tony died last night.'

"I asked her what happened, and she went on to tell me what had taken place. I was heartbroken. I just didn't want to believe it…that Tony was gone.

"After I got myself together, and off the phone with Pam, I woke up Steve and told him about Tony and what had transpired. We didn't tell our daughter at the time because I wanted both of us to tell her together. We knew it would be difficult for her. She adored Tony, as did so many others. Our children claimed Tony as a 'big brother.' He was trustworthy and spent more time doing activities and playing sports with our son, Steven, and Lil' Tony, who are only a year apart in age. Tony and Lysa trusted us, and we trusted them.

"The next Sunday at church, I kept looking up in the sound room, looking for Tony to show up. My heart went out to Lysa and the boys."

—Carolyn Liggon, Family Friend and Member of Bethesda New Life Gospel Church

"Tony was an amazing person. I met him in the late eighties. I dealt more with his mother, who was one of the teachers at the church. As Tony grew in his faith and attended church regularly, we started spending more time together, as the older men did with the young men as mentors. He was a jokester. Tony showed interest in serving and was given the responsibility for the media department, including managing the music recording and playing the drums. One of the ongoing jokes was about his orange car we called the 'general.' The car was old and would break down when it overheated, but he loved the 'general.'

"I'm a little strange when it comes to grief. I just get busy and do stuff, so I can deal with it. That's what I did. I would see what the pastor needed, you know, see what Lysa needed. And I remember telling her [Lysa], 'You have everyone around you now. It's not going to get hard until everybody leaves. Then there's one thing that you have to do.' When asked what that was, I said, 'Live.' I, and some of the guys from church, would play basketball every Saturday morning around nine o'clock at Hamilton Junior High School or we'd go to the park and play football with the boys. But I kept busy and didn't think about it. I had just written a play [for the church], and Tony was in the play. Carolyn was in it. Lysa was in it, too. The play was entitled, *The Call*, and we had put it on one Saturday evening. I began to write the sequel in my mind that Sunday after. And, losing Tony had affected me so much that I stopped writing for a long time. I never picked up a pen to write the sequel, even though Lysa had given me permission to write it because everybody in the play was a tight-knit group. It wouldn't have been the same without Tony.

"You know the first thing we do is ask God, 'Why?' But the bottom line is that the Lord knows what He's doing. And He had planned it before He even created everything that day. He already knew what would happen at that time. I think those things are the things that, you know, you hate to say it, but it brings out the best in each other. And it brings out unity. We may not understand, but you have to live on afterward."

—Steven Liggon, Family Friend and Member of Bethesda New Life Gospel Church

Tony was an inspiration to many. Family and friends delighted in his presence. He brought out the best in people. His charm and sense of humor were two of his best qualities. He had an undercover charisma that you wouldn't see coming, as with his jokes. He made such a significant difference and had a profound impact on the lives of those who knew and loved him—family, friends, and firefighters alike. If you knew Anthony, you knew he was a true, dedicated friend who you would say lived to serve and inspire. We will cherish the time we had with him and will never forget the difference he made in our lives.

CHAPTER
Eight

When One Is Hurt, We All Are Hurt…
When One Is Lost, We All Are Lost

*B*eing a firefighter requires commitment. The training and dedication to carry out the duties can be arduous, but purpose-filled and rewarding. Yet, firefighters are very much like extended family members. After working together in high-pressure situations for shifts lasting up to twenty-four hours, they forge special bonds of trust and friendship unlike other relationships. They meet each other's families, share holiday meals, and talk about each other's lives. They see and experience things on the job the average citizen wouldn't be able to handle. Sometimes, they are attached to a tragic event or an individual as a matter of reverence, but in every case, they represent the highest level of commitment that an organization can ask of an individual or team.

When One Is Hurt, We All Are Hurt... When One Is Lost, We All Are Lost

As public servants, they encounter situations that challenge their resolve and dedication to the oath they swore to uphold. Their willingness to perform is seldom, if ever in question when the ravages of fire or other emergencies strike or directly affect their loved ones. So, when one is hurt, they all will hurt. When one is lost, they all are lost.

The following snippets from the June 4, 1999, article from *The Washington Post* speaks volumes to how the loss of life in the line of duty affects fellow firefighters, loved ones, and the city as a whole.

"A young DC firefighter in his dress blues, standing outside Bethesda New Life Gospel Church, crumpled to the ground and wept. Moments before, Rep. Steny H. Hoyer (D-Md.), sounding like a Baptist minister, had begun speaking of D.C. firefighter Anthony Phillips, who died in a townhouse blaze on Sunday.

"Fire can burn the body and suck the breath from our lungs. But it cannot steal our souls," Hoyer said. People inside the Northeast Washington church clapped and shouted, "Hallelujah!"

Outside the church, the field was covered with grief. There stood a nearly silent sea of dark blue made by hundreds of uniformed members of "the family" of firefighters, from all the Washington area companies and from others as far away as Buffalo [New York].

The front doors of the church were closed even before the 10 a.m. funeral began because every one of the 420 seats was taken. Mourners filled the overflow room to the side of the chapel, content to hear the sweet hymns and eulogies. The firefighters stood outside, gathered around speakers or under one of the eight tents that offered the only shade.

The truck that Phillips rode—now stenciled with his nickname, "Sauce," at the bottom of the door where he stood on Sunday—waited in the church parking lot to carry him one last time. He was eulogized at the church he loved, an unassuming brick chapel at 750 Kenilworth Ave. NE, just off Interstate 295. The marquee outside said, "God Bless You, Brother Tony Phillips. Rest In Peace. We Miss You."

Phillips became a member of the church at age 14 when he sang in the Youth Chorus and served on the usher board. Later, he joined the Kings of Faith gospel group, studied the Bible and was a mentor to young men through the Men's Fellowship Ministry.

D.C. Mayor Anthony A. Williams (D) recalled a story about Phillips showing up for work on his first day "sporting his engine jacket" with his nickname at the time, "Hot Sauce," already on it. "Apparently, no one had bothered to tell him the cardinal rule of nicknames: You're not allowed to pick your own."

Phillips's punishment was to be taunted with other names—"Mayonnaise, Mustard, Ketchup—anything but 'Hot sauce.'" Finally, everyone settled on "Sauce," Williams said.

Raymond Sneed, president of the D.C. Fire Fighters Association, explained: "He loved to eat, and in large quantities. He had a reputation for putting hot sauce on everything."

Out on the lawn, a woman in dress blues rubbed the shoulders of a fellow firefighter, who bowed his head and wept. Another woman held up her firefighter husband each time his body went limp with grief.

President Clinton sent a message, passed out to those in attendance, which in part said, "Sacrificing all to safeguard the well-being of others, firefighters Phillips and Matthews represent what is best about America."

When One Is Hurt, We All Are Hurt...
When One Is Lost, We All Are Lost

Later in the day, a steady procession of weary firefighters, many still in their formal blue suits, moved through another line to view the casket of Matthews at St. Paul Baptist Church in Capitol Heights.

This was after they had hoisted the glistening casket of Anthony Sean Phillips, Sr. onto the truck of Engine Company 10, where his charred hat and size 11 boots stood at the back. This was after the hour-long procession that went through the city, stretching from Northeast to Southeast and Southwest, passing his old fire station on Florida Avenue, where a line of his co-workers saluted and a big silver bell rang out.

Then Phillips passed one last time before the people he served and served beside. Past the dozens of flashing firetrucks and ambulances and cars at every intersection. Past the intersection of Minnesota and Pennsylvania Avenues, where someone tossed red chrysanthemums at the casket.

Over the Anacostia River, where the rescue boats flashed their lights and shot arching fountains of water into the sky. Past the children gathered outside Peabody Elementary School, who waved and saluted. Past the middle-aged white man on Maryland Avenue who held a small American flag and a hand-painted sign that said: "Thank you."

And the middle-aged black woman on Bladensburg Road who held the barely legible handwritten sign: "God Bless The Phillips Family." And the crowd in front of the Fort Lincoln townhouses, where Phillips died trying to save someone's property. There, elderly and young stood ramrod straight with their hands over their hearts.

And finally, to Fort Lincoln Cemetery, where just outside the gates, people lined one side of the street and two firetrucks formed an upside-down "V" with the American flag hanging between them, flapping in the wind."[6]

"I guess, every now and then, you'll think of something... about the good things. We had this book we kept in the firehouse called the *Quote Book*. When guys would make stupid statements, it would get written down in the book for posterity. There was a statement in there from Tony: *Man, I stink so much, I don't know how my wife sleeps with me.* That is still in the book to this day.

"That's what I think about when I think about what happened. I don't dwell on the bad things. I think about him being funny. I remember he came into the firehouse one day and made a peanut butter and jelly sandwich because we just had that around. He made his sandwich and loaded it up with jelly. As soon as he took a bite, it dribbled down the front of his shirt. Everybody started taking shots at him, all in fun. He was good about it.

"I'm not going to sugarcoat anything. There's always been racial tension in the fire department, but I've never seen such a group of people get together and support each other all for a common cause. I still get choked up thinking about it. Just phenomenal—male, female, black, white. Never experienced anything like that when I was in charge. People I didn't even know were reaching out to me."

—*John Burger, Former Captain of Engine 10 (1999)*

---

[6]Gaines, Patrice and Allen Lengal. "Firefighters, District Bury Fallen Hero." *The Washington Post*. June 5, 1999. p. B1.

When One Is Hurt, We All Are Hurt...
When One Is Lost, We All Are Lost

"My impression of the Phillips family was that they had a very strong faith and that was the most important factor for Lysa as she coped with that most difficult situation. There were so many question-and-answer sessions regarding what and how the proceedings of the viewing and funeral should be executed. I know the most important concern was to comply with the family's wishes.

"The members of Engine 10 and Truck 13 were nothing short of amazing. They took care of everything from making sure the children had cereal and milk to adding a deck on their house. The Fire Department was just as amazing. They ensured we had everything we needed. All we had to do was ask and it was there. Every evening, the Fire Department had a briefing on the progress and to address any changes or additions. These meetings usually went late into the night. Captain Burger and I never went home until after the funeral. It was all so consuming. I remember Assistant Fire Chief James Martin and many others were truly dedicated to the whole process.

"The tragedy probably affected me like many others. It felt like walking on eggshells or waiting for the other shoe to drop. I know it was on my mind on every fire call for a long time. Eventually, the emotion of the incident released its grip and I enjoyed the remaining portion of my career. Line of Duty Deaths are the ultimate incidents. I think we all put ourselves in the situation and think, *That could have been me.* When it happens to the company you are assigned and just a few hours after you had been relieved from duty, it takes on a whole different meaning. Eventually, we all returned to our aggressive approach to fighting fires. When it's your time, it's your time. The Fire Service is dangerous by nature. We take the risks and accept the close calls and consequences. We accept it as part of the job."

—John Faulkner, Retired Firefighter, Engine 10 (1999)

"I had never worked with anyone who passed away. So, when Tony died, it was devastating…to us all. It changed the laws, the job, the way things were done.

"Tony and I were on the waiting list for a long time to get into the department. It took me eight years of waiting, and I believe it took him seven years. That's a long time to wait for anything, so that speaks to how much we wanted it.

"Tony was a character. He was funny. He would dance around. He would just say things that would make you laugh. Some things I don't even think I can repeat, but he was funny. Even if you got mad at him, you couldn't stay mad. He wouldn't let you.

"In the firehouse, there are only but so many beds and he and I shared the same bed during our different shifts. One time, I remember going upstairs to see him lying in the bed with no sheet and wearing his running pants and boots. The boots we wear are dirty. So, I started yelling about him being on the bed with his boots, and he looked at me and said, "Man, I'm sorry. I'm really tired." He had a look about him that did not allow you to stay angry. He just had that way about him. He had a calmness about him. If he was ever angry, you never saw it. He was just a nice, funny dude."

—James "Gordo" Gordon, Firefighter, Engine 10 (1999)

When One Is Hurt, We All Are Hurt... When One Is Lost, We All Are Lost

"It was late at night. I remember getting a call; when you hear the phone ring at twelve o'clock at night, in most cases, it is not a good thing. William Austin, a friend, and also a firefighter at the time, called to tell me that a friend of mine had been killed in a fire. I couldn't believe it. When he told me it was Anthony, it was very hard to accept and believe.

"It had a traumatic impact on me. I thought about the family of Anthony Phillips and wondered how they were going to actually make it. I wanted them to understand it wasn't going to be a one-day or two-day relationship; I just wanted to be in their lives forever. You want to be strong for others, but you're also asking yourself if you have what it takes to actually continue.

"The loss of Tony changed my thought process. I wanted to become an officer if I would remain a firefighter. So, I studied more because of this situation. As I became an officer, I had a little bit more understanding and a little more sympathy for the officers. And we know that in every situation, there is an opportunity to learn something. I think we all learned a lot from this particular situation."

– Patrick Banks, Captain, DC Fire and EMS Department

"The night of the Cherry Road fire; I don't remember the time when the first call came out. Engine 12 left for the call. At the firehouse, I could overhear radio transmissions and a lot of ruckuses...something was wrong. The second alarm came in. That's when they put the Hazmat Unit on it.

"At the scene, I had my gear on and was backpedaling up the sidewalk to see Joe Morgan lying on the ground. I didn't recognize him because he was swollen. They were trying to get his gear off, trying to cool him down.

"As I proceeded inside, they didn't have Matthews in sight. I started doing a search. To my left was the kitchen. It was still on fire. I raced against the wall, searched the floor, ran across to the couch. I found a body, didn't know who it was. He still had the hose line clinched in his arms. As I grabbed him by the shoulder, the goggles came off and as I started dragging him out, the pants were coming off. I didn't know who it was. I thought it was Matthews. As I dragged him outside, someone said, "That's not Matthews."

"It was Phillips. There were two people missing. I tried to gather myself; tried to understand what was going on. I put my mask back on and asked Captain Conner to go in with me. We did another search. I found the second body, which was Matthews—the hose clenched in his arm and facepiece still on. And, Steve Matthews, another firefighter, helped me carry Matthews outside. Phillips was on the way to the hospital.

"They raced Matthews to MedStar. I was really upset. As I was calming down, smoke was overtaking my lungs. I couldn't stop coughing. I went to MedStar, too. After an hour, I was released. That night, back at the firehouse, I learned that Phillips had passed away. The next day, when I was at home, I heard that Matthews had passed away.

"I try my best to cope with it and to pass on what went on to this very day."

– ***Stanley A. Taper, Retired DC Fire and EMS,***
Hazardous Material Unit (1999)

When One Is Hurt, We All Are Hurt... When One Is Lost, We All Are Lost

"I joined the Department in 1990. I was forced into retirement after May 30, 1999. My relationship with Anthony was professional. By working at rival firehouses, most engagements were trash talk and sports talk.

"I suffered second- and third-degree burns over sixty-five percent of my body. I have undergone over forty plus surgeries over the years. I am still recovering from the psychological scars. The physical scars are mostly concealed behind clothing but cover a major portion of my body—the circumference of both arms and legs, back and front torso, and the back of my head. There were some localized facial burns, but God only allows what you can handle.

"The situation had a devastating effect on my personal life and on me professionally. I now have physical limitations that make it a little harder to navigate life. Professionally, I was forced into retirement, which forced me into depression. But, by the grace of God and the beautiful wife He has given me, I was able to prosper through that turmoil and continue to support my family through other means.

"God is all-knowing, and loving, and was right by my side the entire time. Nothing is guaranteed in life and adversity is a part of the life cycle."

– *Joe Morgan, Retired DC Firefighter (1999)*

"The day of the Cherry Road fire, I drove to Atlanta with my girlfriend at the time, who is now my wife, and my dad. After reaching Atlanta, I received a phone call late in the night. The caller said, 'Yeah, it was a bad fire and a couple of guys got hurt from work.' I told him I wasn't at home, and that's when he said it was Tony and a couple of guys from Engine 26. I cut my vacation short and the next day, drove back to DC to the firehouse.

"Tony was a good man. He was a good firefighter and we were forming a friendship. Those two-hour talks in the morning; it was comforting to him to know someone cared about him and was willing to sit down and talk to him about what was happening on his shift, and some of the things that were being done to him. At that time, I couldn't have done anything about it, other than to try to tell him he could report it.

"After the incident, it was a lot of sadness, a lot of sadness…we all felt sad. We lost a firefighter out of our firehouse. As men, we show the tough exterior, but inside, we're still hurting."

—*Kwame Roberts, Captain of Engine 22/Former Firefighter, Engine 10 (1999)*

"On May 29, 1999, I was assigned to Engine Company 10, on Platoon 3. I was assigned with Tony on the back step. We rode together every day. We ate, slept, played in many ways, enjoyed each other's company. Had a love for one another.

"It was a Friday. Tony, Joe, Lieutenant Cooper, and I showed up for work as usual, at o-dark-thirty in the morning. I relieved the guy on the line, Tony relieved the layout, and Joe drove. Freddie [Lieutenant Cooper] was in charge at the time. It was just the four of us taking care of one another. Normally, there would be nine of us in the firehouse.

When One Is Hurt, We All Are Hurt...
When One Is Lost, We All Are Lost

"It was just a normal day. I was due to leave for vacation the following morning, and I woke up that morning feeling a little under the weather. Shortly after breakfast, Freddie Cooper nudged me, asking, 'Won't you go home?' A friend of mine, George Donahue, was a captain and he was acting as the second battalion chief. He [Freddie] was saying, 'Hey, George is in the office. Why don't you call George, see if you can get leave tonight so you can go home, get some rest before you go on vacation tomorrow?' So, I was being a little stubborn. Around lunchtime, I wasn't getting any better, so I called George and asked if there was a relief for that evening. At the time, there was no relief, but he said, 'But for you, let me see what I can do. I'll call you back.' And within a half-hour, he had called back. 'Look, I got someone coming in for you tonight. It's a rookie from 8 Engine.' I said, 'Okay, great, thank you.'

"We proceeded through our day as normal; a ton of medical calls and whatnot. It got to be dinner time. Meals were simple, everything was simplified. We had pasta and meat sauce. We had spaghetti. We enjoyed our dinner and shortly thereafter, the young man who was to relieve me showed up. It was between six-thirty and seven o'clock. I took my gear off the piece. Tony slid across and took my spot, and the young guy took Tony's spot. So, I let Joe, the wagon driver, know that the guy coming was a rookie and to keep an eye on him. I told the guys I'd see them next week, waved goodbye to them, grabbed my stuff and put it away, and drove to my mother's house. I slept on her couch. Sometime after midnight, my brother called and told me I needed to get up;

he was on his way over to get me and that 10 Engine had lost some guys at a fire. Charlie was there almost immediately.

"We pull up on the ramp at the firehouse and as soon as I got out of the car, someone—can't remember who it was—told me we had lost Tony. I was in shock, just in disbelief."

—*Robert Hottinger, Firefighter, Engine 10 (1999)*

My conversation with Firefighter Robert Hottinger was the most emotional discussion I've had during the entire process of interviewing the firefighters. The tragedy and losing Tony haunts him, but to a level of pure heartache and pain. But there were also expressions of the good memories. As he talked about his lost brother, Robert struggled to control the tears and the agony he was experiencing.

He shared with me that Tony took his spot on the fire truck that night because he went home sick. If that change in position hadn't taken place, he wondered if Tony would still be here. This has troubled him throughout the years and continues to trouble him even now.

Coping with the loss of Tony has been a major mental and emotional fight for Robert. Even though he knows he bears no fault in Tony's death, he still wonders if things were different, and if he hadn't gone home, would this have occurred? Or, if he were in that spot, could it have been him being mourned? As I expressed to him, we do not have control over certain things. No one had a clue that "routine call" would lead to this tragedy. Looking at it through my spiritual eye, I told him that I believe, "God picks his best flowers, and Tony, at that time, was His best flower. And you still needed watering from God.

That is why you are still here. God is not ready for you yet." Will he ever heal? I believe he will over time.

My compassion for Robert led me to ask him if he ever considered talking to a mental health professional to help him through his grief. He said he had not. After seeing what he is going through, I highly recommended that he should consider it.

The unsettling effect Tony's death had on him is something that many firefighters deal with at some point throughout their career, which is a form of post-traumatic stress disorder (PTSD). This condition is rarely resolved without professional help.

Although the department offers mental health service for its professionals, it is not utilized as it should. The men and women are not taking full advantage of the benefits. It's difficult going through life trying to fight the things that continue to haunt and cause emotional distress.

Like Firefighter Robert Hottinger, there are many others who have been suffering from the same difficulty of coping with losses as well as in-the-field incidences they have witnessed. It takes special people to do this job, but they are human. There is a limitation on what they can endure. But when it begins to affect you and your daily life and your family, it may be time to seek professional help.

"A merry heart doeth good like a medicine: but a broken spirit drieth the bones." (Proverbs 17:22)

He Answered the Call

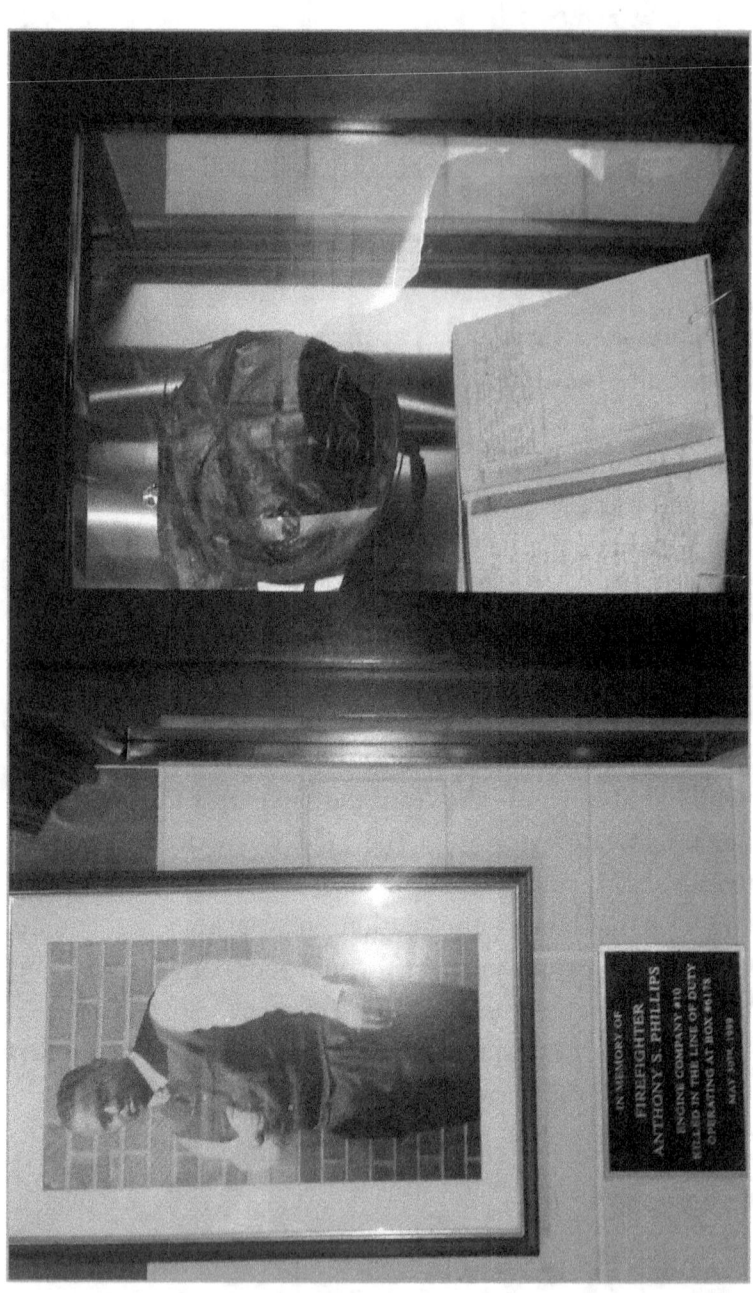

Memorial at Engine 10.

When One Is Hurt, We All Are Hurt...
When One Is Lost, We All Are Lost

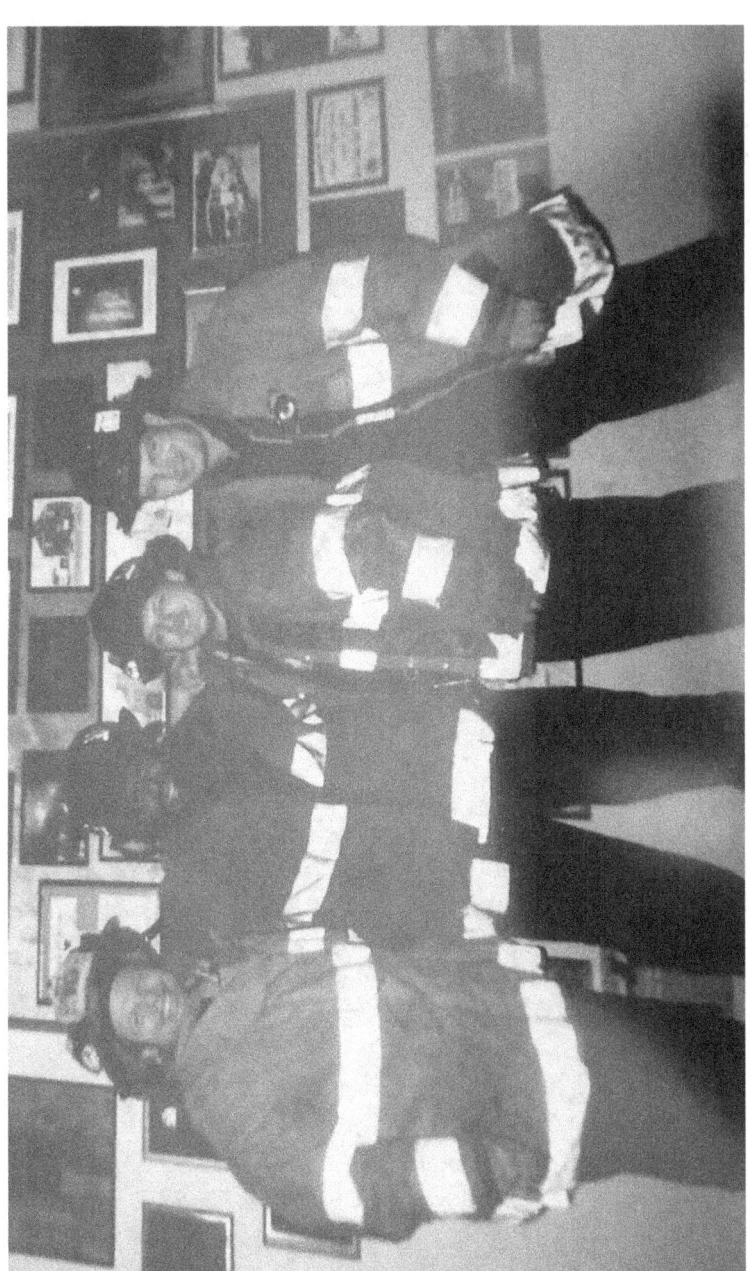

Tony with fellow firefighters of Engine 10.

National Fallen Fighter Memorial in Emmitsburg with Edward Pearson, Retired Deputy Fire Chief–Operations, DC Fire and EMS Department.

CHAPTER
Nine

Celebrating the Life of a Man Who Lived for God—Our Fallen Hero

It took him seven years to achieve his goal of becoming a DC firefighter—a desire he had at an early age to serve his community. I recall the physical emotions Tony showed the day he received the letter to start the training academy. It was as if he had just won millions in the lottery. Then came the time to go through the gruesome six-month training. It was clear that the training was intense when he came home every day exhausted and sore. But he persevered through to the end. "Oh yeah, baby!" as he would say. The time had come for him to take that oath to serve as a firefighter in the District of Columbia Fire Department. He did it! Our family and friends couldn't have been prouder of him. Thus, on many occasions, after the tragedy, when the media asked if I had any regrets about Tony becoming a firefighter, in every instance, my response had always been the same, "I have no regrets. His dream was to become a firefighter and serve. He always said that when he goes, he wanted to go doing what he loved, and that was doing his job as a firefighter." As one of his fellow firefighters, Preston Williams (deceased), said in an interview, "Sauce loved his job, and he said when he goes, he wants to go in a 'blaze of glory'."

Firefighter Anthony Sean "Sauce" Phillips' life and death were not in vain. Firefighters and other individuals from all over the nation as far as Canada came to join family, friends, the community, and local fellow firefighters to celebrate and honor my husband.

Sauce's celebration of life began with an emotional memorial service at Engine 10 on June 2, arranged by his colleagues. The children and I, along with immediate family and friends, arrived at the firehouse where members of the community, the men and women of Engine 10 and other engine companies gathered, offering their condolences and expressing their adoration for Phillips. They were very attentive to us and demonstrated gentleness, particularly to Lil' Tony and Arzel. While this was an honorable thing to do, it was the beginning of an agonizing week for the family, knowing what was ahead of us. Plus, the media was always present, covering every aspect of the memorial service.

On June 3, 1999, there was an all-day review at our place of worship, Bethesda New Life Gospel Church, northeast, Washington, DC. Very early that morning, Captain Burger and Lieutenant Faulkner accompanied the children and I and our family to the church. We had to prepare ourselves and show enormous strength to greet those individuals who would come to offer their condolences. From 8:00 a.m. to 4:00 p.m., family members, friends, and firefighters flowed through the church to pay their respects to our loved one. Those times were set to make it convenient for firefighters from the various engine companies to stop by to offer their commiserations and get a final view of their fallen brother without any disruption to their public service to the community.

Entering the church that morning, surrounded by family and firefighters with Lil' Tony's hand locked into mine and Arzel being carried by his grandfather alongside us, was extremely difficult. There aren't any words to express the pain I felt, not just mine, but for my children, as we approached the casket. It felt as if we were walking in slow motion down the middle aisle of the church and the casket was moving toward us. Suddenly, a burst of throbbing pain came upon me from my head and flowed through my body as we got closer to the front of the church where Tony's body was lying in repose. I looked back at Tony's parents and sister, who were following behind me, and the boys to make sure they were okay. The agony and pain I saw on my mother-in-law's face were incredibly disturbing. She appeared to be completely lost in her emotions. As I reflect, I'm sure she felt as if her life was over, which is understandable. She is a loving mother. Tony was her firstborn and had always been there for her. They had an amazing, unbreakable mother-son bond.

When we approached the casket and had a clear visual of Tony, Lil' Tony squeezed my hand as tears of pain flowed down his little cheeks, and at times, seemed motionless. Oh, my goodness…reality had set in. I reached over and took Arzel out of his grandfather's arms and embraced him tightly.

I could not imagine how he was feeling or if he had any idea what was really happening at that moment. However, he suddenly became very still with a look of despair on his face as he looked at his dad's body. It felt like the beating of his heart was at a standstill. What could I do? Our children were suffering the loss of their dad as I was suffering the loss of my husband and best friend. I had to be strong for them as well as for everyone offering their condolences and expressions of love. I thank God for giving us peace and strength to make it through that day.

While we would have loved to be at the church all day to greet everyone who came by, we were not able to do so. It wasn't possible. I believe we left the church around midday, hoping to get some rest and to prepare for the funeral service the next day, which we knew was going to be much more difficult to withstand. Our support team made sure we were comfortable and well-rested in preparation for the all-day homegoing celebration.

Friday, June 4, 1999, was the day we had to say our final goodbyes to a son, brother, father, husband, friend, a man of God, and firefighter. Oh, Lord, we had to endure the agony of what we experienced the day before to another level. *God, help us!*

Tony's homegoing commemoration was unlike one I had ever seen before for a common citizen. The men and women of the District of Columbia Fire and EMS Department took full responsibility of arranging the memorial service, reviewal, and the organization and management of the funeral service.

When we arrived at the church that morning, I was truly astonished by the number of people I saw from the window of the limousine. It was very inspiring for me to witness how much so many people loved my husband. The parking lot and the property adjacent to the church overflowed with hundreds of people and firefighters from Washington, DC, Maryland, Virginia and several other states, and many as far as Canada, who came out to support our family and honor the life of their fallen brother. My heart bled as I observed what was taking place. There were representatives from the various local media. There were several metro buses parked in front of the church with side displays that read, "In Honor of DCFD Anthony S. Phillips, Engine 10." There were fire trucks everywhere. But as I glanced over to the right side of the church parking lot, I noticed the truck from Engine 10. This was the truck Tony rode to make his last call, and that was the truck that carried his body to the church, would carry his casket through the procession and to his final resting place, Fort Lincoln Cemetery.

After we, the family, were able to contain ourselves, Chief Edwards escorted me, arm-in-arm, into the church, followed by other firefighters as they held onto my mother-in-law and other family members. It was such a numbing moment. I felt like I was walking through a crowd of people with my eyes closed, not being able to see anyone around me.

The sanctuary was at capacity—standing room only. Walking down the aisle of the church toward the casket with our children and family members was such an unnatural feeling. There were beautiful flowers surrounding the casket, the choir was singing glorious hymns, and ministers and dignitaries who were there to pay their respects to our hero congregated on the pulpit. Mayor Anthony Williams

(Washington, DC), Congresswoman Eleanor Holmes Norton (Washington, DC), Congressman Steny Hoyer (Maryland), and the fire chief eulogized Tony, all praising him as a father, husband, friend, and an excellent firefighter whom they will never forget. A selected number of individuals also expressed their sympathy and delivered encouraging words to the family and reiterated to Tony, Jr. and Arzel that their dad was a hero. Our loving pastor, Reverend Iola B. Cunningham (deceased), knew him from a child and led the service. She spoke highly of him, saying, "Tony was exceptionally sincere and devoted to whatever he was asked to do. This isn't a time for sadness, it's not a time to mourn, it's a time to celebrate the life of this man of God." We rejoiced in songs and praises and gave honor to God for putting this wonderful being in our lives as he **"…pressed towards the mark for the prize of the high calling of God in Christ Jesus."** (Philippians 3:14)

The ceremony lasted several hours. Hundreds of people gathered on all sides of the church to view and listen to the service on monitors that were set up by the city, as the church's seating capacity was too small to hold the hundreds of people who came to celebrate the life and memory of our hero. At the end of the celebration, we walked peacefully behind the casket as his fellow firefighters carried it to the firetruck. We all watched in sorrow as the honor guards performed a special salute to Sauce while his fellow brothers placed his casket onto the truck. I stood still, in a disoriented state, trying to understand why this was happening. I was present in a physical state, but so far away mentally.

After all the formalities, we got into our perspective limousines and lined up behind the firetruck in preparation for the procession led by what appeared to be more than fifty police vehicles. Likened to a "procession of a president," as noted by a news media reporter, we were indeed surprised to see how many strangers lined the streets to pay their respects to our fallen hero. All eyes were on the fire engine draped in black with the name "Sauce" along the side. The funeral procession was comprised of more than one hundred vehicles and lasted for miles, taking Tony's body throughout the city and pass the Capitol building. Along the route, much of Washington stood still. As the firetruck slowly approached and paused in front of Engine 10, the dreadful "Last Alarm" bell sounded three times, a custom that symbolized the dedication DC Firefighter Anthony "Sauce" Phillips had for his duty. This special signal represented Sauce having selflessly given his life for the good of his fellow man, his tasks completed, his duties well done; and he's "returning to quarters."

At that moment, I could hear Tony saying in an amusing manner, "All this is for me, man! This is for me!" Although I was hurting, I smiled, knowing he always saw the light in the darkness. I believe he wanted to put a smile on my face and to let me know that everything was okay. I'm sure he was thrilled to see the boats from the fire department paying their respects with a ceremonial water salute as the procession crossed the Sousa Bridge along the Anacostia River. It was an amazing sight and tribute.

As we approached the cemetery, people young and old from the Fort Lincoln and Bladensburg communities lined up along the road in tears with signs of support and sympathy, as this is the community in which Tony lost his life responding to his final call. Enthralled by the outpouring of support, we wished we had the opportunity to roll down the windows to convey our gratitude to everyone.

Located on Bladensburg Road at the entrance of the cemetery, were two ladder trucks, one on each side of the road, its ladders extended in the air, with the US flag waving in the middle, making an overpass for the fire engine to enter the Fort Lincoln Cemetery. That, too, was an amazing sight; and one I am sure Tony would have genuinely appreciated.

As we approached the gravesite, his comrades, family, friends, dignitaries, and the media were all awaiting his arrival. As the pallbearers, his co-workers from Engine Company 10, removed his coffin from the firetruck, weeping and sounds of sorrow echoed throughout the burial ground.

Tony's final resting place, the "Last Alarm Garden," a special section established in memory of Maryland Fire Chaplain Pierce Damewood and dedicated for firefighters and EMS personnel in the Fort Lincoln Cemetery, sealed the fact that my husband and the father of our children was really gone. Pastor Cunningham presided over the burial ceremony also. Representatives from Maryland and the District shared kind words and presented the children, me, Tony's mother with the state and the city flags and other items of tribute. The 'fly-over' by the park police in dedication of this hero and fallen firefighter was one of the most impressive honors bestowed upon Firefighter Phillips for his commitment to serving the community.

Now that Tony was no longer with us, how were we, the family, supposed to live on without him? Anxiety began to set in. Where were we to go from here? What were we going to do without him?

Celebrating the Life of a Man Who Lived for God—Our Fallen Hero

'Our fallen hero,' Firefighter Anthony Sean "Sauce" Phillips, a son, brother, husband, father of two young boys, a man of God, friend, and firefighter, made the ultimate sacrifice. He was only thirty years old.

Celebrating the Life of a Man Who Lived for God—Our Fallen Hero

He Answered the Call

Celebrating the Life of a Man Who Lived for God—Our Fallen Hero

He Answered the Call

Celebrating the Life of a Man Who Lived for God—Our Fallen Hero

He Answered the Call

FIREFIGHTER ANTHONY SEAN PHILLIPS, SR.

October 19, 1968   May 30, 1999

Box Alarm 6178

May 30,1999 began as a "typical day" for the members of Engine 10, #3 platoon, the busiest engine company in the United States. Last year Engine 10 responded to 6,792 emergency calls for assistance. However this morning is unusually quiet. There are only two runs before noon. Perhaps it was due to the heat; maybe, the Memorial Day Holiday. Whatever the reason, the members of Engine 10 weren't complaining. They welcomed the respite however brief.

In the afternoon, firefighter Tony Phillips had some special visitors. Phillips was a four-year veteran of the DCFD and was extremely proud of being a member of Engine 10. His wife Lysa, accompanied by Tony Jr. and Arzel Shamar, made a surprise visit to Tony's fire station known affectionately known as "The House of Pain." They would spend several hours with their "hero"... taking photos, pretending to slide down the fire pole, and climbing over daddy's fire engine.

Tony and Lysa Phillips were married for five years. They had an intense, personal faith in God. Their life revolved around The Bethesda New Life Gospel Church where the entire family was involved in ministry. In a few hours, Lysa Phillips would forever cherish the memories created during this spontaneous visit to Engine 10. Perhaps this visit was divinely inspired.

As Engine 10's tour progressed the runs picked up. By midnight, it had returned to "business as usual" at the "House of Pain"...Fourteen Medical Locals..three Local Alarms...and two Box Alarms

In a few hours Tony Phillips' relief would be arriving and he would make the transition from firefighter to sound technician at New Life Gospel Church. But that was not to be. Two long beeps on the Vocal Alarm shattered the stillness of the early morning hour. The time is 0016 Hours.

Box Alarm ... Engines 26 ...17...10 ...and 12. Trucks 15 ... and 4. Rescue Squad 1, Battalion 1 respond for the report of a house on fire at 3146 Cherry Road, NE.

"Engine 26 on the scene ... smoke showing" Tony Phillips hears the radio transmission from E-26's officer. Tony is right where he wants to be, running the line for Engine 10. In a few seconds he will be where the action is.

"It was his dream to become a fire fighter" Mrs. Phillips told a reporter for the Washington Times. "He always said if he would go, he would like to go doing what he enjoys doing, which is being a firefighter."

As Engine 10 arrives on the scene, the members of Engine 26 have just entered the first floor at the front door and are proceeding down a hallway towards the rear of the house. Firefighter Phillips quickly gets Engine 10's line in service. He was advancing their line to back up the crew of Engine 26.

Suddenly ... conditions deteriorated, and some type of flashover occurred, thereby trapping the firefighters. Brother Phillips, wearing the new SCBA with the integrated PASS device, went down. His fellow fire fighters, realizing something terrible had just occurred and following the sound of the PASS device, quickly located their injured colleague and removed him to the outside. For the previous 18 hours the fighters of Engine 10 and Engine 26 had been administering to the needs of others ... now their efforts were focused on attempting to save the lives of their fellow fire fighters. Brother Phillips was quickly removed from the fire ground and transported to Med Star. Despite heroic efforts by the medical staff at Med Star to save his life, Brother Phillips passed away at 0100 hours on May 30,1999.

Brother Anthony S. Phillips is the 96th member of The District of Columbia Fire & Emergency Services Department to die in the line of duty..

"He wanted to do his job. I have no regrets at all about him becoming a firefighter".
                                        Lysa Phillips

Celebrating the Life of a Man Who Lived for God—Our Fallen Hero

The Capital City Fire Fighter, Memorial Issue

Fire Fighter Anthony S. Phillips
Remembered

DC Delegate Eleanor Holmes Norton

"We are indebted to these brave young men who loved the work of firefighting"

Reverend clergy, Lysa Phillips, the two loving parents who raised this fine young man and other families and friends of Anthony Phillips. Firefighters of Engine Company Number 10, officers and firefighters of the District of Columbia Fire Department, my good friends who serve the District of Columbia as District officials, ladies and gentlemen. Firefighters themselves were the first to embrace this young family. Surely today, the family feels the arms of the entire city around them. In my conversation with Lysa, I have been struck by her personal strength and her inner ease. I have deeply admired how she has drawn on the strong bond and the deep love she and firefighter Phillips shared, and the extraordinary devotion firefighter Phillips had for his children, his family, and his work. So strong was his love for his family, his God, and his work that his love has made them very, very strong.

I know something of the pride of the families of firefighters. I have hanging in my Congressional office in a special place, a picture of my grandfather, Lieutenant Richard Holmes of Engine Fire Company number 4, who lived with DC Fire Department in 1902. Again and again, we are told that firefighter Phillips loved his work. We are indebted to these brave young men who loved the work of firefighting and who, unlike us, neither feared nor shunned the danger but rushed to conquer it. We must not forget that five were injured, two seriously, and that two have died.

This morning we give thanks for the young loving life of Anthony Phillips. We honor him for his courage and his sacrifice. But in remembering firefighter Phillips, we are especially mindful of the men and women of the Department he has left behind to carry on his work of confronting danger whenever and wherever it appears. To properly remember firefighter Anthony Phillips is to remember the members of his Department and their indispensable mission, the debt we owe him and the debt we surely owe to them.

Rep. Steny Hoyer D-MD

"Fire can burn the body but it cannot steal our soul"

To the family who loved Tony and who Tony loved; Lysa, Anthony Jr., Arzel, his mom, his step-dad, his aunts, his uncles, his sisters and brothers, I am pleased to join you. I am not pleased at the occasion, but I'm pleased to join you. Mayor Williams, Chairman Cropp, members of the Council, Chief Edwards, Chief Ramsey, my own chief, president of the representatives of these two brave young men and the three others - Ray Sneed of Local 36; the International Association of Fire Fighters, my good

friend Al Whitehead, so many others that I could mention. I don't know whether any of the family of

He Answered the Call

Louis Matthews are here, but we remember them and him as well, as we join you.

One of the most difficult things that I or any public official does, is to join with others in lamenting the loss of those who serve our community, particular those in the Police and Fire service. It is a difficult task because it is invariably saying good-bye to good and decent men and women who died before their time defending our community, our lives, our homes and those we love. It is difficult because we lose too many firefighters in this country. Last year alone, we lost 91. Anthony, I think, is the 96th DC firefighter we have lost down through history, Mr. Mayor. We know that as long as we have dedicated individuals, dedicated to protecting our community, that we will never, ever, stop adding names to the fallen firefighter memorial located in Emmittsburg, Maryland.

The fact of the matter is, as all of us in this congregation knows, that fighting fires is a dangerous business. As I noted, we lost 91 firefighters in this country last year, including DC firefighter John Carter - actually in the latter part of '97. Over 40,000 firefighters were injured, many of them seriously, responded to the calls for help from all of us, black and white, rich and poor, young and old. Like the Armed Forces or our police, firefighters put their lives on the line every time a call goes out. And indeed, firefighters and police every morning they get up they make a determination to go to work, to be ready to respond, they know, at least as you do, that there might be a day like this.

And so it was with Anthony Sean Phillips Sr., thirty years of age. How very young, how too soon to go. He died in a way tragically, but in another way, heroically last Sunday. He, along with firefighter Louis Matthews and his colleagues at Engine 10 and Engine Company 26, became the 95th and 96th firefighter to give their lives in defense of the citizens of the District of Columbia.

And, as a representative not from the District of Columbia, but of our community at large - as Mayor Barry and I used to talk - on behalf of those who visit the Nation's Capital as tourists, workers, shoppers, businesses. I didn't know Anthony Phillips personally, but I've read so many great things about him. He must have been, and you know so well, a remarkable individual.

I'm told that Anthony had three loves in his life. The first, praise God, was his personal relationship with Jesus Christ. Lysa, I don't know because I didn't get the chance to talk with you, but it was my wife at eighteen who led me to the Lord. And I don't know whether that was the same with you, but if it was, God bless you. Anthony has died, but John 3:16 tells us, "Whosoever believe in him shall not perish, but have eternal life." Fire can burn the body but it cannot steal our soul.

The second love of his life was his family, Lysa and his two young sons. I saw, and Eleanor saw as we sat here, Mr. Mayor and Linda, the family come by and others come by and hug Lysa, and hug the children, and hug the mom. Many of us have been there on the day of the funeral, many of us have been there even a couple of days after. But Lysa as we hug you today, and hold you today, and lift you up, and share your grief and sorrow, let us all commit that, as I know the fire family always does, that we'll be there next week and next year and next year.

And he loved the fire service. It was not just his job, but his passion and the fulfillment, as I understand it Lysa, of a boyhood dream. I don't know how many of you know, but Anthony had to wait seven long years on the register before being hired. Seven years he waited to serve. Anthony Phillips was not one of the famous of the world, but Anthony and Arzel, let me tell you, he was one of the heroes of the world. He used each day the Lord gave to him in such a way to advantage those in our community who knew him and the overwhelming majority of those who didn't know him. We thank God that other brave men and women will step forward to fill the vacuum left by the deaths of Anthony and Louis. Our domestic defenders the fire service and our police are an absolutely critical component of our free society. A critical component of our free society. Without them, we could not have this civilized society.

Brother Reinhart, you said correctly that this was a celebration of life. It is, and the good news is, it's a life that lives on with God.

Celebrating the Life of a Man Who Lived for God—Our Fallen Hero

Mayor Anthony Williams

"Our community has a responsibility to the children. Not only to be role models and friends in the time of need, but also to help them, to help them keep the memory of their father alive" ———

Let me thank you for having us here today. Bishop Cunningham, the wonderful choir of Brother Rinehart. It's a wonderful rendition. I think all of you have helped usher Anthony to a higher place and a better place. We all thank you for that. Our distinguished leaders, our firefighting community, thank all of you for having us here today because it means a great part of the celebration of life and to celebrate the life of a fallen hero. Today is not just a day of mourning, it's also a day of remembrance. It's a day of sadness and remembrance, but also a day great pride. Since I heard this news on Sunday, and all of us heard it, it's been difficult for us to express all of our thoughts and all of our feelings. Like all of the citizens the District, my heart, and all of our hearts aches at this loss and our prayers go out to the families and the loved ones. But I think at this time that we remember and say a prayer for Louis Matthews and his family and for Joseph Morgan and his family.

Joseph is fighting for his life right now, so let us pray for him.

But today we honor fallen comrade Anthony Phillips whose sacrifice touches us all, because like his colleagues Anthony had never met the people who lived in the house he was fighting to save. He fought against that fire as it were his own home with his own wife and his own children trapped inside. He did what he had always done and what all firefighters do: they did their duty without hesitation, without fear, without thought of recognition. That's who he was. The quintessential firefighter devoted to his community, his family, and to his God. In life he represented everything that is good and honorable about public service. In his passing he reminds us of the finality of our own existence and the nobility of sacrifice for others. The firefighters of Engine Company 10 know who Anthony Phillips was. He was hero, he was a father, he was a husband, he was an outstanding firefighter, and he was a friend.

On the day the fresh young firefighter showed up for work sporting his engine jacket, and here they had a joker on their hands. The jacket read, as I understand it, 'Hot Sauce'. Apparently, no one had ever bothered to tell Tony that the cardinal rule of nicknames is, you're not allowed to pick your own nickname. So for the rest of the week his name was 'Mayonnaise', 'Mustard', 'Horseradish', 'Ketchup', anything but 'Hot Sauce'. But Anthony, who eventually settled for the name 'Sauce', didn't mind the teasing and he learned to give as good as he got. He had found a second home in Engine Company 10. He became a part of the family. He cared about his colleagues and he shared his life with them. He even sang to them, even when they didn't want to hear it. And he loved sports, in particular he loved the Dallas Cowboys, but nobody's perfect.

Tony was bragging after he and some buddies had won a decisive victory in a basketball game, he said, "We crushed them dudes," he told his friends. But somehow in telling the story, he had left out the fact that he was opposed by 7th graders. That was vintage Tony. Always looking on the bright side, never discouraged, never down and never angry. He was one of those people who carried so much joy, so much heart on his sleeve, it can't help but rub off on others.

One of the recipients of that joy was a young man from the neighborhood named Jabar. Jabar had been coming around the fire station for a number of years as many young kids, and when Tony met him, he took the young man under his wing. Tony was a role model and he was an understanding friend. He made an impact on Jabar through the power of his caring and through the size of his heart. Tony's children who have lost their own father are going to need that same kind of love and support from all of us. Our community has a responsibility to these children. Not only to be role models and friends in the time of need, but also to help them, to help them keep the memory of their father, keep the memory of their father alive.

Anthony Jr. and Arzel, you will always know your father was a hero. He was an important man and he was willing to make the most profound sacrifice anyone can make. To Lysa, we can only express our gratitude to you on behalf of the people of our city and our community. We will never forget what your husband did. To Mrs. Saunders, there is no greater pain on this earth than saying good-bye to a child. I know that words can't express the grief that you feel. The people of this city owe you a debt that cannot be repaid, because you raised a fine man. You raised a man of compassion and love. You raised a hero.

So we will not forget this man. Tony has left this life, but his spirit will live on the lives that he touched. It began in the firehouses, the firefighters consoled one another, it's continued in this church. It must go on tomorrow, as Steny Hoyer has said, day after, and day after, and day after. The book of John tells us that there is no greater love than to lay down one's life for one's friends. No greater love. That's the love that Tony Phillips showed every day. It's the love and commitment that all our men and women in uniform give to us as they put their lives on the line to make our communities safe.

And so on this day as we wish this hero peace, we wish him godspeed, let us say a prayer for Tony for his children and for his family, for all those who serve and for all those who risk their life for us. On behalf of a great city, and on behalf of a great community, thank you Tony.

City Council Chairman Linda Cropp

"There is no greater gift or no sacrifice that one human being can give than his willingness to lay down his life to help others."

First giving honor and glory to God. To the Revered clergy, to the friends, to the men and women in blue who are firefighters, to the family, to the parents, to wife Lysa, to Tony's children, Anthony Jr. and Arzel. Good morning. I am joined here with colleagues on the Council, Council member Vincent Orange, Sharon Ambrose, Phil Mendelson, and Harold Brazil. We come here today to share your grief and to celebrate the life of Anthony Phillips.

Have you ever seen a mosaic, a puzzle? You know how it comes in all these little pieces, and if you look at the pieces individually, you see different colors. Sometimes the piece of the mosaic doesn't tell the whole story. Have you ever noticed that? But somehow when you lay it out in a pattern, a story is told. You see a beautiful picture. Today, Lysa, children, parents, look around; you see the mosaic of Anthony Phillips. You see, he came to be the center part, today, of this puzzle. And you see picture of a life of service to many. Separate pieces, but coming together to tell a wonderful story.

It is with a heavy heart that I join with you today to recognize and honor and praise firefighter Anthony Phillips. Our prayers are with the family, friends and colleagues of this courageous young man. Today, we come together to remember and honor, we come together to celebrate a life. We come together to comfort each other, and we come together to lay a perpet-

ual base upon which you Lysa, and your children and your parents can come in the future. We also raise our hearts in a healing prayer to the family of firefighter Louis Matthews who also gave his life in service to this city; and to firefighter J.A. Morgan and to firefighter Lieutenant Charles Redding and their families, they sustained injuries in this tragic fire.

This tragedy occurred early in the morning on May 31st. This proximity to Memorial Day is significant. Memorial Day is a day which our entire nation has set aside to praise and to honor special people, heroes. A hero has been described as someone who reacts continuously with no regard to their personal safety but to help someone else. Firefighter Phillips and Engine Company 10 are indeed our heroes. Heroes are not based upon age, for he was a young man.

Instead, heroes are determined by those things of which character is made. Anthony Phillips character was the material of heroes. There is no greater gift or no sacrifice that one human being can give than his willingness to lay down his life to help others.

Lysa, you have demonstrated such love, strength and grace in the face of tragedy. You have been a role model to all of us. Thank you. Thank you on behalf of the citizens of the District of Columbia. May you, and the parents, and your children, be sustained by God's

Celebrating the Life of a Man Who Lived for God—Our Fallen Hero

enduring love. It is our hope that our words - as Eleanor, and Steny, and the Mayor, and those who will follow - that our words will bring you comfort. That the silence of many of the others who are here, will also give you comfort by the knowledge that they are here and that they are giving out rays of love to you. And memories, memories of a smile, of a husband, of a father, of a friend who will give you continued solace. It's these memories of Tony that you should not use to dwell in the past, but to help you to create a bright future. I wish that we could mandate an easy path for you. You know, sometimes those of us in political life think that we can mandate everything. But we cannot. But there is a greater power, a greater power that can mandate on earth, and that power is God. And in God there is comfort, peace and assurance that the sun shall rise tomorrow. With God as your partner, little Anthony and Arzel can be lifted to brighter future. The Lord will give strength unto his people with peace, it is told us.

So Anthony Sean Phillips, the mosaic of which you were a part is still here.

Have you ever noticed in that mosaic, in that puzzle that has of all of these other men and women who are willing to give their life; the puzzle of his church, the puzzle of his family. Have you ever noticed that when you see that whole picture, when you take one picture out that the puzzle is still standing and still there, and the picture is still there and the form is still there. And that is what we have today. We still have the picture of life that Tony created. And even though that piece was removed, the form is still there, and the beauty of the picture will be there forever. May God give you peace.

Fire Chief Donald Edwards

"Tony was running the line for Engine 10. Engine 10, he's running the line for God now. He's riding Engine 10 up there."

Members of the clergy, honored and distinguished guests, Mrs. Saunders and the Phillips family, good morning. This is a good morning. When I came into Bethesda this morning, I was indeed sad. But Brother Rinehart lifted me up. This combined choir behind me, you brought some joy into me today. Somebody just said, "Some sho nuff joy". It was. It has helped me today.

Early Sunday morning, my telephone rang, and it rings often as the fire chief of this city. This time they were telling me there was a house fire and there were several firefighters down, so I immediately got up and proceeded to the fire ground. On arrival, all of the engines had been removed, the fire was out. It was evident that the District of Columbia Fire Department had done what they were required to do.

However, Engine Company 10 and Engine Company 26 were going home lesser a number of people. At that point I went into my little corner and I thought about what I had to do as the leader of this department, and I was immediately surrounded by other fire service members. Father Smith the chaplain of the Department of the Police and Fire Chaplain Service was there with us. I sent him and one of my deputies to pick up Lysa. I didn't know Lysa. I knew Tony only from the fact that he was a member of this agency, but I knew I had heard of his dedication. We shared some common things.

One, the nickname 'Sauce'; that was a name that I had years ago when I worked at the Post Office, and I'm not going to tell you what it meant. He was a native born son, such as myself. He, too, was a graduate of Theodore Roosevelt High School, like myself.

So, even though he was slightly younger than I, there was some connection there.

The first members of the family to arrive at the hospital were his mother and his step-father and, of course, they were distraught. Shortly thereafter, Lysa came

He Answered the Call

and she too, quite naturally was distraught. But I sensed something there. I sensed strength.

And it has been verified during the last four to five days. This family of people, this family, I mean they if you want to know what family is about, talk to these people.

Anthony was a true role model. He was first and foremost a son, he was a husband, he was a father and an excellent firefighter. He filled that role model to the max. He was and always will be one of us. My wife made a remark to me on Monday, I believe, or Tuesday after Lysa had her press conference at Engine 10, and I was overwhelmed by the degree of strength that this lady showed. This is a 26 year old woman who stood tall, has been standing tall. And my wife told me, "There's a lot of church in there." That's what she said. She told me, "There's a lot of church in there." That was what I sensed on the early Sunday morning sitting up in Washington Hospital Center. It takes a woman to define those things for us sometimes.

To the many men and women in blue that are seated, those that are lined up outside, that have come to share our grief, don't grieve for Tony Phillips. Let's celebrate the life of Tony Phillips. This a celebration. This is indeed a home-going service for not only a servant of man but a servant of God. On the night of his death, Tony was running the line for Engine 10. Engine 10, he's running the line for God now. He's riding Engine 10 up there.

On Sunday during the day, I went back to the scene of this tragedy, just to survey the scene in an attempt to see what happened. We don't know what happened, but we will attempt to find out. But as I looked out there in the parking lot and I saw a female standing off to the side weeping silently. She had on a firefighter uniform, but it wasn't the District of Columbia. So I went over to her and she identified herself as a member of the Prince George's County Volunteer Fire Department. She served as a chaplain or assistant chaplain. She said she just had to come. And she gave me that I'm going to I'm going to read. The author is unknown, but the title is "The measure of a man".

Not how did he die, but how did he live
Not what did he gain, but what did he give
These are the units to measure the worth
Of a man as a man, regardless of birth
Not what was his station, but had he a heart
And how did he play his God-given part
Was he every ready with a word o good cheer
To bring back a smile, to banish a tear
Not what was his church, not what was his creed
But had he befriended those really in need
Not what did the sketch in the newspaper say
But how many people were sorry when he passed away.

It is evident that Anthony Sean Phillips Sr. filled all of those roles. Anthony, God speed. Thank you.

Good Morning, Lysa, Tony, Jr, Arzel, Mrs. Saunders, family, friends and fellow fire fighters.

Local 36 President Ray Sneed

"Tony was proud to be a D.C. fire fighter and proud to be a member of the busiest Engine Company in the United States, Engine Company 10."

Today the Nation's Capital is covered by a veil of sadness. Two of our bravest, Firefighters Anthony Phillips and Louis Matthews made the supreme sacrifice while fighting a fire in a town house at 3146 Cherry Road, NE.

As we gather today to celebrate the life of Brother Phillips, please continue to keep Brothers Joe Morgan

Celebrating the Life of a Man Who Lived for God—Our Fallen Hero

and Charlie Redding in your thoughts and prayers. Brother Morgan remains in critical condition at the Washington Hospital Burn Center. Brother Charlie Redding was released from the "Center" and is recovering from his burns at home.

If our worship service here today at Bethesda New Life Gospel was a typical service, Tony Phillips would be "on duty", in the balcony, sitting behind the sound board making sure that the soloist, the choir and the speakers, all sounded their very best. But then this is not an ordinary service and Tony's dedication and commitment to this church will be sorely missed.

Tony Phillips attempted to live his life according to Biblical Principles. His priorities were his Lord, his family and his profession. Tony Phillips poured his heart and soul into all three priorities.

He loved being involved in this church, he referred to it as "his church". As a teenager Tony sang in the youth chorus, ushered and was a mentor with the Men's Fellowship Ministry. But, the ministry he was most proud of was his knowledge and ability to operate the audio/visual equipment.

Tony Phillips was a family man and proud of it. Just hours before his passing, Lysa, Tony, Jr. and Arzel spent several hours at Engine Co. 10, taking photos of the children doing what all kids want to do when they visit a fire house, pretending to "slide down the fire pole" and climbing all over their daddy's fire engine.

Tony was proud to be a D.C. fire fighter and proud to be a member of the busiest Engine Company in the United States, Engine Company 10. His fire house is affectionately known as "The House of Pain".

Tony loved to "run the line" for Engine 10. This is the fire fighter who literally advances the hose line into the burning building, locates the fire, then opens the nozzle and extinguishes the blaze. Obviously this is a very dangerous assignment. Early Sunday morning Tony Phillips was running the line for Engine 10 at 3146 Cherry Road, NE.

Tony loved to eat and in large quantities. He had a reputation for putting hot sauce on everything. This resulted in his nickname of "Sauce", short for "Hot Sauce". As the procession passes by, take a close look at Engine 10 and you'll see the word "Sauce"

newly stenciled on the crew cab door where Tony Phillips rode on his last alarm.

Several days ago I visited with Lysa, the children and Tony's mom. I went to their home to assure the Phillips family that Local 36 will always be part of their extended family and to see if they had any immediate needs. We talked about Tony, his love of fire fighting, his church, his family and how proud he was to be a member of Engine Co. 10.

Lysa and Tony's mom shared with me his excitement upon learning of his assignment to Engine 10 during graduation from the Fire Training Academy. He kept repeating, "Engine 10, Engine 10, I'm going to Engine 10." He was a happy fire fighter. Tony Phillips had finally realized his goal of becoming a D.C. fire fighter. His seven-year wait to be appointed was finally over. He was now probationary Firefighter Anthony Phillips of Engine 10.

Ladies and gentlemen, ours is a dangerous profession as evidenced by our being here today. Every year approximately 100 fire fighters lose their lives protecting their communities. Others are forced onto the Disability Retirement rolls as a result of career ending injuries. Any thoughts that our profession is easy or mundane can be easily dispelled by a visit with Firefighter Morgan at the Washington Hospital Burn Center.

Unfortunately, as D.C. fire fighters we have been down this road before. When Brother John Carter was killed in the line of duty 18 months ago promises were made, yet when the FY 2000 Fire Department budget was released, those promises were broken.

To the elected leaders of the District of Columbia and Fire Chief Edwards, please don't use this tragedy as a forum to make statements which are politically correct and appeasing, indicating you are going to recommend additional staffing and increase funding of the Fire Department budget knowing full well you have no intentions of following through with such promises.

To the Phillips and Matthews family, I am holding firm to my belief that some good will come out of this tragedy and the supreme sacrifices made by Brothers Anthony Phillips and Louis Matthews will be the catalysts for positive change.

He Answered the Call

The Capital City Fire Fighter, Memorial Issue

Lysa, Tony and Arzel, we are and will always be family, and as family we will always be there to insure that your needs are met.

A verse of scripture found in Matthew 25:21 sums up Tony Phillips' life. .....

"Well done thy good and faithful servant, thou hast been faithful over a few things, I will make thee ruler over many things, enter into the joy of thy Lord."

Firefighter Anthony Phillips
of
Engine Company 10

Rest in peace.

The Washington Post
Wednesday June 2, 1999

Two Firefighters Gone

The sight of black bunting draping Engine Company 10 and Engine Company 26 tells you that something terrible went wrong. The D.C. Fire Department is a sadder place today as a result of a double loss-the death of two firefighters in a single blaze. A firefighting tragedy of that magnitude hasn't occurred in the District since 1911.

As of yesterday, investigators were still trying to determine what started the fire early Sunday in the basement of a Fort Lincoln town house in Northeast Washington. This much is known. Firefighter Anthony Phillips, 30, a four year member of Engine Company 10 was in the living room of that house, along with Louis Matthews, 29, an eight-year member of Engine Company 26, and two others: Joseph Morgan Jr., 36, and Lt. Charles Redding, 41.

All four had rushed into the burning home, looking for someone who might still be inside, when within seconds-the living room became engulfed in flames. The inferno was brought on by the explosion of gases superheated from fire in the basement below.

Veteran firefighters call the blast a "flashover." Hell on earth is more like it.

Lt. Redding was treated and released from the hospital Monday afternoon. Joseph Morgan remains hospitalized in critical condition with burns over more than half his body. Anthony Phillips, who always wanted to be in the action, was dead in less than an hour after the explosion. Louis Matthews, another highly regarded firefighter, died Monday afternoon. The couple who lived in the house had scrambled to safety before the four firefighters arrived.

It all happened so quickly. One moment, everything at the scene is going as it should; the next, a disaster. And yet with all that uncertainty and risk, today and tomorrow and for days to come, firefighters-a breed unto themselves-will continue taking on dangers that the rest of us avoid at all costs. That is why this city will pause to honor Anthony Phillips and Louis Matthews later this week. They may be gone, but their legacy of bravery, unselfish service and sacrifice will live on.

CHAPTER
Ten

Coping After Everyone Has Moved On

The service is over, your loved one is resting in peace, and everyone is gone. What do you do? How do you cope and move forward? *Coping with the loss* of a loved one may be one of the most difficult situations one will endure. The grief can be extremely intense, leading to great sadness and even depression—something I am truly familiar with. Although grieving is part of the healing process to help overcome the feelings of hurt, it can also be a time to embrace the memories of our loved one.

It is a fact that death is a natural part of life. However, everyone reacts differently to death and uses various coping mechanisms to manage their grief. While most people may be able to recover from a loss on their own with time and support, others may require help from a mental health professional. No one can determine the length of time one should grieve. Everyone has a certain level of resilience, which may determine how long they endure or struggle with the loss.

Coping and moving on with life without Tony was exceedingly difficult, but it forced me to develop a renewed sense of purpose in life. However, the heartache never ends.

There are many strategies our children and I have used over the years to cope with the death of my loving husband and their brave dad, including engaging in conversations about him and what occurred on that night God called him home. We reminisced about the good and funny times we had with him with family and friends. I focused my time and attention on the children and kept them engaged in activities to help divert their attention to other things. Prayer was always my outlet. Overall, we learned to accept that he would no longer be here with us physically. But the most unusual coping method, as some may see it, was and still is, "the fly." Yes, the fly!

Let me explain. The day of Tony's funeral, I was in our bathroom curling my hair in preparation for the service. Suddenly, from out of nowhere, I heard a buzzing sound. A fly had flown into the bathroom and landed directly on the mirror in front of me. I smiled. I had an instant internal feeling of comfort, as if I knew he was there with me.

Without thought, I said, "Tony, of all things, you decided to come back as a fly." So, I began to communicate with the reincarnated Tony, the fly. Weird? No. It felt natural to me. "I know it's you, but why did you have to leave us?" As the tears streamed down my face, I kept repeating, "What are we going to do? What are we going to do?" I continued to talk to the fly. It did not move off my mirror the entire time until I left the bathroom. The saying, "I would like to be a fly on the wall," was clear here. But Tony was no doubt, the "fly on the mirror."

Several years later, I moved from our home into another house several miles away. Low and behold, the fly began to appear in the bathroom in my new home, and still does; particularly when I am going through personal trials and tribulations. It is as if he knows I need him at those moments. I get so excited when he appears. As soon as I hear that buzz, I know he is there to listen to me and to let me know he is there with me through the good and not-so-good times. Some may think that is strange, but it is real for me. I have shared this with my family. So now, when they see a fly in their homes, they let it be, as they consider the possibility it may be Tony. *Closure.*

Getting closure does not happen overnight. However, for me, it occurred during the night. Several months after his death, I realized I needed to get the children involved in activities to keep them active and focused on other things as they grieved. Lil' Tony being the oldest, and one who loved sports, I enrolled him in a youth football league.

Every night, for two weeks, I battled with a dream in which I asked my husband and best friend to come back to us. The football field appeared as the setting in my dream. In every dream, I asked him to come back. "I don't want to come back. It's peaceful here." His continued response comforted me in knowing he was where he belonged. He had conquered the prize. **"Blessed is the man that endureth temptation: for when he is tried, he shall receive the crown of life, which the**

Lord hath promised to them that love him." (James 1:12) And that was when I accepted that my husband was at peace in the arms of his Heavenly Father. *Closure.*

The unlimited support we received from family and friends was more than what we expected. There was always someone there for us, whether church members, firefighters, or family who would call to check-in or stop by to sit and talk about Tony, looking back at their experiences with him. People were always there to make sure we were okay. Help was always near. The stories we shared always left everyone laughing, feeling better, and thanking God for putting him in our lives. The late Thomas Moore (1779–1852), an Irish songwriter, singer, and poet wrote, "Earth hath no sorrow that heaven cannot heal." I embraced those words, as it ministered to my spirit and helped relieve the pain during my time of lamentation. *Closure.*

Endless communication about their dad, including talking about his death and how much he loved them, and sharing things about him they did not know, was effective in the healing process for the boys and for me. We talked about the things they have in common with him, which were more than they'd realized. From their hairlines to their laughter to their handwriting. Their calm spirit and respectable manner. Their kindness to others and their procrastinated ways are some of the behaviors they've inherited from him. Sharing some of this with them helped validate their identity with their dad, spawning *Closure.*

Viewing photos of Tony and me from when we began our relationship up to his thirtieth birthday celebration with the boys stirred endless jokes and laughter, as they couldn't believe that our hairstyles and clothing were so very different back then. With their crazy sense of humor, the photos of their dad and his friends taken at the Go-Go were even more hilarious. It shocked them to see us in our younger days, in which they'd commented, "We forgot that you were once our age. We've only known you as our mom." There were also many photos they didn't remember taking with their dad. But seeing them, more so for Arzel, reassured him that his dad was always there. *Closure.*

Visits to the grave site, whether together or alone, throughout the years has also helped us to achieve *Closure.*

Family at the cemetery.

I didn't realize I was still in such misery until I set out to write this book. I realized I had much more healing to do. Uncovering all the media footage I received in 1999 of the daily coverage from the day of the incident to the funeral service, photos, and other items I had stored away, exposed more emotions than I had experienced in years. It was likened to digging in a wound after it has somewhat healed, which could be more painful to endure.

The first time I visited the home on Cherry Road was eerie, yet therapeutic. The current owner, Mr. Smith, welcomed me into his home, where my husband's spirit enveloped me. It's difficult to explain that moment in words. Our conversation, his statements of encouragement and inspiration, and seeing the inside of the home gave me a sense of relief. I am glad I mustered the courage to go to the place where my husband completed his task and fulfilled what God had called him to do. *Closure.*

After meeting with Mr. Smith, I contacted the original owner, Mrs. Naughton, whom I had never met or spoken with, and told her I was authoring the book. I asked if she would meet with me to get her narrative about what occurred and how she had managed throughout the years. I didn't know what to expect or how our conversation would go. We had a relaxed dialogue. Our exchange ended serenely. I spoke with the person who owned the home where my husband completed his final call. *Closure.*

I reflected on May 1, 1999, when Tony and I were a part of a play entitled, *The Call*, that told the story of a young lady [me] who suddenly lost her loved one. I had an overflow of support from people as I was going through my loss. But after a while, those people moved on, and I was alone to grieve on my own. There were few people around to help me cope. As I meditated on the correlation between the play and Tony's passing, I believed that God orchestrated the play to prepare me for what was to come. That production occurred twenty-nine days prior to Tony's passing. *Closure.*

Surrounding myself with people who poured positivity into my life, including my Christian family, was very influential in my healing. They helped keep my spirits up and my focus on God. When I felt discouraged, they prayed for me and with me. When I felt weak, they lifted me up. When I felt as if I couldn't go on, they carried me. Their prayers and reassurance gave me the strength to get through my tough days and nights. But their unwavering love and compassion upon us was instrumental in coping with the loss of our loved one. As noted in Matthew 18:19, **"Again I say unto you, That if two of you shall agree on earth as touching any thing that they shall ask, it shall be done for them of my Father which is in heaven."** *Closure.*

In conclusion, my faith has always been my foundation. Giving my life over to Christ at an early age and my growth in the Word of God has enabled me to cope in peace over the years. The thought that Tony and I grew in Christ together also kept my heart still. Even though it's been a struggle and an emotional toll, God continues to comfort me. When my mind revisits that dreadful time, I cry out to God and ask Him to hold me. And He's always heard my call. I know that God doesn't make mistakes. I have accepted that He has chosen one of His "best flowers." Death is an appointment we must all keep. *Closure.*

"Blessed be God, even the Father of our Lord Jesus Christ, the Father of mercies, and the God of all comfort; Who comforteth us in all our tribulation, that we may be able to comfort them which are in any trouble, by the comfort wherewith we ourselves are comforted of God." (2 Corinthians 1:3-4). *Closure.*

He Answered the Call

CHAPTER Eleven

Planning for the Unavoidable

Who thinks about preparing for one's own death or of our family members? We live life as if we will be here on earth forever. Every day is our day. We expect to wake up each day, and that's how we believe it's supposed to be. However, that is so far from the truth. We have no control over what occurs in our lives daily. We are born, we live, and we die—all in that order. Death is unknown to any of us, but we know we will leave this earth when it is our time. Yet, we do not think about what we need to do to prepare for that inevitable day. Who wants to think or talk about death? No one does, but we must.

Tony and I never had an in-depth conversation about preparing for death. We owned property and had children, but neither one of us had a Last Will and Testament. We rarely talked about death, much less to discuss our own. At such a youthful age, we didn't think about it. As children of God, we understood about life and death, and death is unavoidable. However, no one knows when that day will come.

With becoming a firefighter, the dangers of the job became more real to Tony. He knew he was going into a dangerous field, but he had a purpose to fulfill.

One day, at the start of May 1999, as we drove by a funeral home on Rhode Island Avenue, Tony talked to me about the dangers of the job. He opened the dialogue with, "Just in case something should happen to me, I've made sure you and the boys will be okay…" My immediate response was, "Boy, what are you talking about? Nothing is going to happen to you." That was not a conversation I wanted to have, not at that moment, and, to be honest, not ever. We were too young to talk about death. We both had our whole lives ahead of us, so we thought. Besides, nothing would happen to him. At least, that's what I thought and what I believed.

Tony disclosed the various benefits the department offered and what was in place if he died in the line of duty. He also talked about HEROES, Inc., the organization that helps to support families of fallen firefighters and police officers and the financial contribution he'd made into their scholarship program to help further the children's education. The more he talked, the more distant my mind wandered. I didn't want to hear or move further with that conversation.

At the end of the month, God called Tony home. Who knew that the discussion he attempted to have with me was to prepare me for this day? Did he have an inkling? It did not dawn on me that God had orchestrated the conversation. If he had not shared that information with me, I would not have known how he prepared for his family.

The experience of the sudden loss of my husband opened my eyes to how important it is to prepare for death, and that includes preparing a will. Even though he was my husband and I was the mother of our children, there were many legal hurdles I had to overcome to receive the benefits that were in place for the children and me. Without a will, everything went into an estate, and I had to go through the legal process to be executor of my husband's estate and named the legal guardian of our children because there was no will.

I thank God for Engine 10's former Captain John Burger, our family liaison, and Lieutenant John Faulkner, who assisted him, and all the people who helped and guided them through the general and legal process for my family. Without them, I am not sure how I would have gotten through it. I am sure it was challenging for Burger and his team to work through all of this for me. They did all the legwork. All I had to do was sign paperwork. My God, I am grateful for them! But that goes to show why it is important to have a will, whether you're married, unmarried, or in a dangerous line of work.

A will is a legally binding document that gives you control of what happens after you depart this life. It includes who you designate as an executor (who will carry out your wishes), the beneficiary(ies) (who you want to inherit your assets), instructions on how and when the beneficiary(ies) will receive the assets, and who will have guardianship of your minor children.

It makes managing your assets and the process clear and easier for your family and anyone involved. Without a will, the state in which you live decides how to distribute your assets to your beneficiary(ies), according to its laws. The resulting settlement process may not produce the outcome you would prefer for your family. You can prevent this from happening by having documents drafted that reflect your wishes. If you don't have a will in place, there is no guarantee people will follow your wishes.

Lessons learned! After my loss, I made it a priority to meet with an attorney to prepare a will. I implore all adults with family and property to do the same. Tell your family your end-of-life wishes in writing, so the process will be easy for them to follow.

"Therefore be ye also ready: for in such an hour as ye think not the Son of man cometh." (Matthew 24:44)

Conclusion

Whether you knew Anthony "Sauce" Phillips, or maybe not at all, I hope his story and the information shared in this book by his loved ones and firefighters speak volumes of the sacrifice men and women in civil service professions make to save lives and protect their communities. They put their lives on the line daily, performing selfless acts and fulfilling their duties without hesitation.

Becoming a firefighter and serving the community was Tony's dream, and it came to fruition, which was an extremely exciting time in his life. I never knew of anyone more fixated on becoming a DC firefighter than him.

Dying in the line of duty was not what we expected to happen to my husband, nor were we ever prepared for such a tragedy. He aspired to serve until retirement. God had a different plan. I've learned that we have no control over our lives, as it is not our own. God giveth life and God taketh it away when our work on earth is done.

Tony's life and death were not in vain. He had a significant, positive influence on everyone he met. His comedic ways kept you in stitches. His friendship was genuine. His ability to give valuable advice was one of his strengths. His "nobody bothers me" and calming ways were contagious. His desire to learn and eagerness to execute motivated others. And those who benefited deeply appreciated his generosity. But most of all, his faith and love for God defined him.

Sauce's call to glory had a profound impact on so many lives. The Word of God shared during the celebration service reassured mourners that our lives are not our own, something Tony witnessed to others during his Christian walk. Following the service, many gave their lives over to Christ. Tony so let his light shine before men, that they saw his good works, and glorify his Father which is in heaven (paraphrased: Matthew 5:16).

Tony's life spoke for him. The Bible says in Romans 2:11, **"For there is no respect of persons with God."** I believe He will take one life to save many, and that's what He did.

Tony was never ashamed of living a Christian life. He died doing what God had called him to do. This wonderful son, brother, father, husband, firefighter, and man of God fulfilled his purpose. **"But glory, honour, and peace, to every man that worketh good…"** (Romans 2:10)

Our family extends immeasurable gratitude to the members of the DC Fire Department, in particular, Engine 10 and Local 36 for their commitment to always be there for

Conclusion

the family of their fellow brother. We appreciate you. May God continue to keep watch and protection over you and reward you for your good deeds.

Now, on this book's publication day, May 30, 2019, the 20th Anniversary of the "Fire on Cherry Road, NE," my sons and I honor DC Firefighters Anthony "Sauce" Phillips (Engine 10) and Louis Matthews (Engine 26) for the sacrifices they made to the "call to duty," and to both of our families and friends as we continue to mourn our loss. Also, we would like to express our admiration to Firefighters Joe Morgan (Engine 26), Lieutenant Charles Redding (Engine 26), and Stanley Taper (Engine 12, Hazardous Material Unit) for their heroic acts. We thank God for restoring you back to health from the severe injuries you sustained from this tragedy and the pain and suffering you endured during your recovery. God bless you!

A Soldier Gone Home

A son, brother, father, and husband dear,
Loving friend to all near,
A soldier gone home,
No more battles to fight,
God took you with him on a heavenly flight.
We love you, we miss you,
For you were always there,
Now there are no more burdens for you to bear.
May you rest in peace inside heaven's gate,
Where all your loved ones for wait you.
—Author unknown

IN MEMORY OF

FIREFIGHTER ANTHONY S. PHILLIPS

ENGINE COMPANY #10
KILLED IN THE LINE OF DUTY
OPERATING AT BOX #6178

MAY 30TH, 1999

In Memory Of...

In Memory Of...

He Answered the Call

The State of Maryland

Governor of the State of Maryland, to

ANTHONY PHILLIPS
"POSTHUMOUSLY AWARDED"

, Greeting:

Be it Known: That on behalf of the citizens of this State, in recognition of a man whose courage, commitment and strong sense of duty should serve as an inspiration to his colleagues, friends and fellow citizens... in honor of the true professionalism that he demonstrated as a member of the District of Columbia Fire and Emergency Medical Services Department and as the citizens of Maryland join with the people of the District of Columbia in expressing our condolences, gratitude and great respect for the memory of a brave and honorable man who lost his life in the line of duty, we are pleased to confer upon you this

Governor's Citation

Given Under My Hand and the Great Seal of the State of Maryland, this 3rd day of June, One Thousand, Nine Hundred and Ninety-nine.

Parris N. Glendening
Governor

John T. Willis
Secretary of State

In Memory Of...

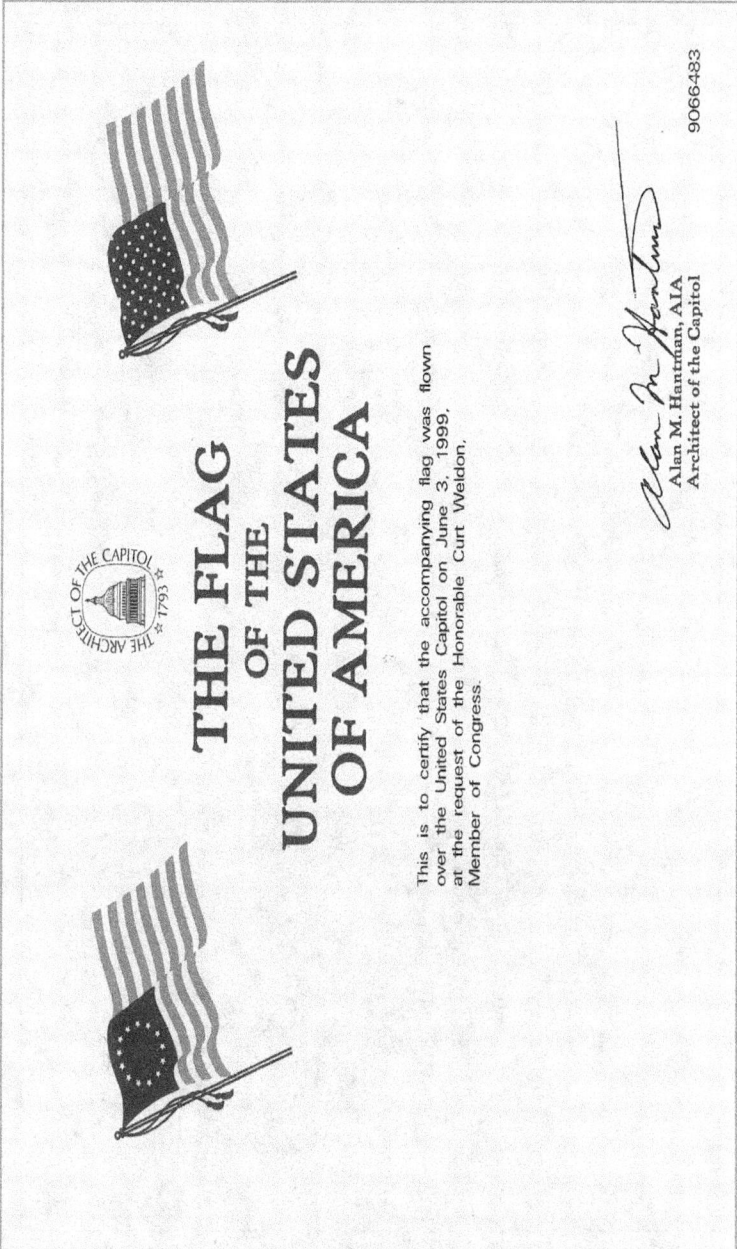

MARYLAND STATE FLAG

This flag was flown over the State House in Annapolis, Maryland and is presented to the family of

Firefighter Anthony Phillips

in recognition of the courage, devotion to duty and uncommon sacrifice exhibited by Firefighter Anthony Phillips during the performance of his duties. His selfless actions were in keeping with the highest standards of the District of Columbia Fire and Emergency Medical Services and his memory will serve to uphold the noble traditions of his profession.

Maryland's flag bears the arms of the Calvert and Crossland families. Calvert was the family name of the Lords Baltimore. Crossland was the family name of the mother of the first Lord Baltimore. The escutcheon or shield in the Maryland Seal bears the same arms. This flag in its present form was first used about 1886, and was officially adopted in 1904.

Parris N. Glendening, Governor

John T. Willis, Secretary of State

June 1, 1999

In Memory Of...

BETHESDA NEW LIFE GOSPEL CHURCH MEN'S MINISTRY

Reverend Iola B. Cunningham, Pastor

Deacon Stephen A. Liggon, Sr., President

June 4, 1999

Behold, how good and pleasant it is for brethren to dwell together in unity!

It is like the precious ointment upon the head, that ran down even Aaron's beard: that went down to the skirts of his garments;

As the dew of Hermon, and as the dew that descended upon the mountains of Zion: for there the Lord commanded the blessing, even life for evermore.

Psalm 133

To the Family of Anthony Sean Phillips, Sr. "Tony"

We the Men's Ministry of Bethesda New Life Gospel Church, wish to extend to the family our condolences in your loss. We too feel this loss, as Tony was a big part of our Ministry. He was a lively part of it and believed in it's unity. He did not miss an opportunity to help out where ever he could. He brought laughter and joy into the lives of those he touched.

We hope that the family takes solace as we do in knowing that Tony was a saved young man and that he has gone on to be with the Lord. We know that he has taken his place with Jesus and is smiling on all of us who continue to keep the faith and run the race that he has already completed

Lovingly Submitted,
The Men's Ministry
Bethesda New Life
Gospel Church

He Answered the Call

BETHESDA NEW LIFE GOSPEL CHURCH
750 Kenilworth Avenue, N.E.
Washington, D.C. 20019
(202) 388-7995

BISHOP IOLA B. CUNNINGHAM
PASTOR and FOUNDER
(202) 397-8040

Trustees
Harry Byers, Jr., Chairman
George S. West, Asst. Chairman
Wydenia Saunders, Secretary
Stephen Liggon, Treasurer

Church Secretary
Daffney Archer
(301) 599-9328
Date Clerk
Pamela McFadden
(301) 322-4151

Friday, June 4, 1999

OFFICIAL CHURCH PAPER

On Sunday, May 30, 1999, Trustee Anthony S. Phillips, Sr., departed this life to be with the Lord.

Trustee Phillips was a dedicated servant. He became a member here at Bethesda in 1982. Trustee Phillips served faithfully as a member of the Youth Chorus, Usher Ministry, Kings of Faith, and the Men's Fellowship Ministry. He was also one of our percussionists, and President of the Audio/Video Ministry.

Approximately five years ago, Bro. Tony Phillips rededicated his life to Christ. The Lord put running in his feet and placed a desire in his heart to be a blessing to his Church family and to those he came in contact with. Bro. Tony was a great mentor to many of our young boys in the Church and in the community. They looked up to him and respected his guidance. As Bro. Tony developed a hunger and thirst for the Word of God he began to seek him by attending Bible Class and asking questions. He was also a faithful member in our Worship Services. Sometimes he would come directly from the Fire Station to Church and other times he would come to our Church Service and go directly to work.

The Audio/Video Ministry was birthed by Bro. Tony with the permission of his Pastor. He had a yearning to learn all he could. He took classes and visited other Ministries to obtain vital information in order to produce a quality sound system for our Services and to produce quality tapes so that many people could be blessed by hearing the Word in song and hearing the Preached Word of God.

Bro. Tony portrayed Christ in that he loved his family as Christ loves the Church. He was always willing to help wherever he could. Although he was quiet and reserved he had a side that was bright, cheerful and full of laughter.

We all love Bro. Tony dearly, but we know that God loves him best.

To the family we say, be of good courage for earth has no sorrow that Heaven cannot heal.

**DONE BY THE OFFICIAL BOARD OF THE
BETHESDA NEW LIFE GOSPEL CHURCH**

In Memory Of...

COUNCIL OF THE DISTRICT OF COLUMBIA
WASHINGTON, D.C. 20001

June 2, 1999

Mrs. Lysa Phillips
7506 Garrison Place, N.E.
Hyattsville, MD 20784

Dear Mrs. Phillips,

    I offer my sincerest condolences to you and your two small children, Anthony Jr. and Arzell, on the tragic loss of your husband Anthony. Firefighter Phillips' bravery in the face of such danger is to be commended. I am very appreciative for all that your husband did to selflessly protect the citizens of the District of Columbia.

    It is my hope that you find some measure of comfort in the support of family and friends during this difficult time. You and yours are in my thoughts and prayers.

                                Sincerely,

                                Carol Schwartz
                                Councilmember, At-Large

CS/js

He Answered the Call

COUNCIL OF THE DISTRICT OF COLUMBIA

WASHINGTON, D.C. 20001

(202) 724-8052

CHARLENE DREW JARVIS
Councilmember-Ward 4
Chairperson
Committee on
Economic Development

Committee Member
Finance & Revenue
Education, Libraries
and Recreation

June 2, 1999

Mrs. Lysa Phillips & family
c/o: Office of the Fire Chief
1923 Vermont Avenue, NW Room 220-S
Washington, DC 20001

Dear Mrs. Phillips:

    I am deeply saddened about the passing of your beloved Anthony. You have my deepest sympathy. While I know that this is a difficult time for you, please know that my prayers and those of this community are with you.

    Today, I salute Anthony for the service he provided to protect the citizens of the District of Columbia. He will be sorely missed. To the Phillips family we appreciate your lending Anthony to the community which he served as firefighter.

    In memory of Anthony, enclosed is a contribution to the *Firefighter Anthony Phillips Memorial Fund.* May your faith sustain you. I hope it helps to know how many share your sorrow.

With sympathy and understanding,

Charlene Drew Jarvis

Charlene Drew Jarvis
Chair Pro-Tempore
Councilmember, Ward 4

In Memory Of...

[Congressional Record (Bound Edition), Volume 145 (1999), Part 9]
[Extensions of Remarks]
[Page 12295]
[From the U.S. Government Publishing Office, www.gpo.gov]

IN MEMORY OF FIREFIGHTER ANTHONY PHILLIPS, ENGINE COMPANY NO. 10, NATION'S CAPITAL

HON. ELEANOR HOLMES NORTON
OF THE DISTRICT OF COLUMBIA
IN THE HOUSE OF REPRESENTATIVES

Tuesday, June 8, 1999

Ms. NORTON. Mr. Speaker, in my conversation with Lysa Phillips, the very young widow of Firefighter Anthony Phillips, I have been struck by her personal strength and her inner peace. I have deeply admired how she has drawn on the strong bond and deep love she and Firefighter Phillips shared and the extraordinary devotion that Firefighter Phillips had for his children, his family, and his work. So strong was his love for his family, his God, and his work that his love has made Lysa and his family especially strong.

Again and again, we are told that Firefighter Phillips loved his work. We are indebted to brave young firefighters, like Firefighter Phillips, who love their work and who, unlike us, neither fear nor shun danger, but rush to conquer it. We give thanks for the young, loving life of Anthony Phillips and we honor him for his courage and his sacrifice.

In remembering Firefighter Phillips, we are especially mindful of the men and women of the Department he has left behind to carry on his work of confronting danger whenever and wherever it appears. To properly remember Firefighter Anthony Phillips is to remember the members of the District of Columbia Fire Department and their indispensable mission, the debt we owe him, and the debt we owe them.

He Answered the Call

COUNCIL OF THE DISTRICT OF COLUMBIA
WASHINGTON, D.C. 20001

June 4, 1999

Ms. Lysa Phillips and Family
7506 Garrison Road
Hyattsville, M.D. 20784

Ms. Phillips:

It is with heartfelt sympathy that I write to offer my condolences to you, Anthony Jr., Arzel, and the rest of your family. Your deep sense of loss is shared by the people of the District of Columbia.

Since October of 1995, Anthony risked his own safety countless times to protect District residents. Never one to shy away from danger, Anthony's final act was in service to our city. The District of Columbia has lost a hero. We must move forward cautiously, always preserving Anthony's legacy of service and commitment. Both Anthony Jr. and Arzel should continue to take pride in their father's dedication and devotion to public service.

Please know that you are all in our thoughts. If I can be of any assitance to you or your family, please do not hesitate to call.

Sincerely,

David A. Catania
Councilmember At-Large

In Memory Of...

FIRE FIGHTERS ASSOCIATION

LOCAL No. 36
INTERNATIONAL ASSOCIATION
of FIRE FIGHTERS

DISTRICT OF COLUMBIA
2120 BLADENSBURG ROAD, N. E.
SUITE 210
WASHINGTON, D. C. 20018-1498
CODE 202 635-8500
FAX 526-2986

RAYMOND SNEED
President
DANIEL DUGAN
1st Vice President
KENNETH M. COX
2nd Vice President
JOHNATHAN SNEED
3rd Vice President
RICHARD L. MOORE
Treasurer
JOHN R. HARNEY
Secretary

Dear Ms. Phillips:

The Officers & Members of the Firefighters Association of Washington D.C., Local-36, wish to extend our deepest sympathy & express our condolences following the tragic Loss of your husband, Firefighter Anthony S. Phillips. Our prayers are with you.

Sincerely,

Raymond Sneed
President

Affiliated with AMERICAN FEDERATION OF LABOR and CONGRESS OF INDUSTRIAL ORGANIZATIONS
METROPOLITAN WASHINGTON COUNCIL

He Answered the Call

THE
NATIONAL
FALLEN
FIREFIGHTERS
FOUNDATION

16825 So. SETON AVE.
P.O. DRAWER 498
EMMITSBURG,
MARYLAND
21727

EXECUTIVE DIRECTOR
Steve Robinson
(301) 447-1365

OFFICERS
Gerard F. Scannell *Chairman*
National Safety Council

Hal Bruno *Vice Chairman*
ABC News

Steve Robinson *Secretary/Treasurer*
Department of the Interior

BOARD OF DIRECTORS
Fred Allinson
National Volunteer Fire Council

Mary Ann Gibbons
Maryland State Firemen's Association

Arthur Glatfelter
Volunteer Firemen's Insurance
Services, Inc.

L Seth Statler
U.S. Department of the Treasury

Alfred Whitehead
International Association
of Fire Fighters

Rita Wilson
Allstate

FIRE SERVICE COMMITTEE
Chief Neil Svetanics, *Chairman*
St. Louis Fire Department

June 1, 1999

Chief Donald Edwards
District of Columbia Fire and EMS Department
1923 Vermont Ave.
Washington, DC 20001

Dear Chief Edwards:

On behalf of the National Fallen Firefighters Foundation, I want to offer our condolences to you and your department on the death of your firefighters Louis Matthews and Anthony Phillips.

Congress created the Foundation in 1992 to honor America's fire heroes and to remember their families. A grateful nation will honor your firefighters at the 19th Annual National Fallen Firefighters Memorial Service scheduled for October 2000 at the National Fire Academy in Emmitsburg, Maryland. At an appropriate time, you and the families will receive more information on the Memorial Weekend sponsored by the Foundation and the Federal Emergency Management Agency.

In the meantime, the Foundation offers year-round support for the families. Under a Department of Justice grant, the Foundation has established a variety of support programs for fire service survivors. We would like to contact the families in a few months with more information about these support programs. I have enclosed a pamphlet that describes the programs we provide for families.

Please let me know if we can offer any other assistance. Our thoughts and prayers are with you, the Matthews and Phillips families, and the members of your department.

Sincerely,

Steve Robinson
Executive Director

Enclosure

In Memory Of...

COUNCIL OF THE DISTRICT OF COLUMBIA

WASHINGTON, D. C. 20001

HAROLD BRAZIL
Councilmember-At-Large

June 4, 1999

Ms. Lysa Phillips
7506 Garrison Road
Hyattsville, Maryland 20784

Dear Ms. Phillips:

I write to express my condolences regarding the loss of Fire Fighter Anthony Phillips. While I know this is a difficult time for your family, I want you to know that the prayers of the community are with you.

Fire Fighter Phillips conducted himself bravely and heroically. He is an outstanding representative of the District of Columbia Fire and Emergency Medical Services Department.

May the healing grace of God be with you and your family.

Sincerely,

Harold Brazil

He Answered the Call

HOUSE OF REPRESENTATIVES
WASHINGTON, D. C. 20515

ALBERT R. WYNN
Fourth District
Maryland

June 1, 1999

Mrs. Lysa Phillips & Family
7506 Garrison Road
Hyattsville, Maryland 20784

Dear Mrs. Phillips:

I want to express my sincere condolences to you on the death of your husband, Firefighter Anthony Phillips. Bereavement is so personal that few of us, unless we have experienced it ourselves, can comprehend its grief. Mr. Phillips' death certainly is a tremendous loss and our only recourse at moments like these is the power of prayer.

I know that these are difficult times and words cannot heal or take away the pain that you feel. However, I hope you can take comfort in knowing that the loving memories your husband has left behind will keep him close and dear to your hearts. May your faith in God give you strength during this period of sorrow. Also, please know that you have friends and neighbors who stand ready to lend a helping hand.

In this regard, I will continue to keep you in my prayers. If I can be of any assistance, please do not hesitate to contact me.

Sincerely,

ALBERT R. WYNN
Member of Congress

NOT PAID FOR AT GOVERNMENT EXPENSE

In Memory Of...

COUNCIL OF THE DISTRICT OF COLUMBIA
WASHINGTON, D.C. 20001
(202) 724-8045   (202) 724-8055 Fax

SANDRA C. ALLEN
Councilmember-Ward Eight

Committee Member
Consumer & Regulatory Affairs
Public Works & The Environment
Local & Regional Affairs
Human Services

*Sympathy and Condolences
to the Family of*

ANTHONY PHILLIPS

June 4, 1999

The Ward Eight Community, My family and I wish to express our deepest sympathy in the loss of Anthony. Let us not forget that God's love is always with us, His timing is perfect - even in death and we can find comfort in remembering that:

"Forever is too far to see from where we stand today, But loved ones who have reached the end of their journey have found a perfect home."

We know that God's love is always with you, His grace will protect you and His mercy is everlasting. As you pause to reflect on Anthony's life, may you gain inspiration and courage to meet the challenges of life encountered from day to day. Simply know that there are many people thinking of you not just today, but always. May the Lord keep you in his care and bring you peace in the days ahead.

Sincerely,

Sandy Allen

Sandra C. "Sandy" Allen
Councilmember Ward Eight

He Answered the Call

WASHINGTON SPORTS
& ENTERTAINMENT

ABE POLLIN
Chairman of the Board and
Chief Executive Officer

June 4, 1999

Mrs. Lysa Phillips
c/o Bethesda New Life Gospel Church
750 Kenilworth Avenue, N.E.
Washington, D.C. 20001

Dear Phillips Family:

On behalf of the Washington Wizards, Washington Mystics and Washington Capitals, we would like to express our sincere condolences to your family. Your loss of a husband and father has touched our hearts deeply. The City has lost a hero, one who served our community well and has been and will continue to be a positive role model.

We would like to invite Anthony, Jr., Azrell and family out to a basketball or hockey game of their choice. We have enclosed a team-autographed basketball from the Wizards and Mystics, and a hockey puck autographed by Peter Bondra of the Washington Capitals. We hope these items will give you some joy during this very difficult time in your lives.

Please contact Sashia Jones to make arrangements for your visit to MCI Center at 202-661-5000, ext. 4520.

May God be with you.

Sincerely,

Abe Pollin

Enclosures

MCI Center • 601 F Street, N.W. • Washington, DC 20001 • 202-661-5050 • Fax 202-661-

In Memory Of...

THE PRINCE GEORGE'S COUNTY GOVERNMENT

OFFICE OF THE COUNTY EXECUTIVE

Wayne K. Curry
County Executive

June 4, 1999

Mrs. Lysa Phillips
7506 Garrison Road
Hyattsville, Maryland 20784

Dear Mrs. Phillips:

On behalf of the citizens of Prince George's County, please accept my deepest condolences on the loss of your husband, Anthony. We are never prepared for the loss of a loved one who has shared our lives, hopes and dreams. But, I know your memories, family and friends will sustain you during this difficult time. Your sons, Anthony, Jr. and Arzell will also be a great source of strength and solace.

The men and women of the Prince George's County Fire/EMS Department share your grief and hold you and your family in their thoughts and prayers. The dedication and commitment of Anthony in his role as a District of Columbia firefighter are shared by those who risk their lives everyday in service to the citizens of our communities.

Once again, my deepest sympathies to you and your family. My prayers are with you.

Sincerely,

Wayne K. Curry
Wayne K. Exeuctive
County Exeuctive

14741 Governor Oden Bowie Drive, Upper Marlboro, Maryland 20772
(301) 952-4131
TDD (301) 925-5167

He Answered the Call

THE WHITE HOUSE

WASHINGTON

June 25, 1999

Mrs. Anthony S. Phillips
7506 Garrison Road
Hyattsville, Maryland 20784

Dear Mrs. Phillips:

    Hillary and I extend our deepest sympathy on the loss of your husband. Anthony S. Phillips will be remembered for his devotion to duty and steadfast regard for the safety of his fellow citizens. We hope that your sorrow will be eased by the love and support of your family and friends.

    Our thoughts and prayers are with you.

Sincerely,

In Memory Of...

THE WHITE HOUSE
WASHINGTON

June 1, 1999

    With deep sorrow, Hillary and I join the citizens of our nation's capital and the members of the International Association of Fire Fighters in paying tribute to the memory of fire fighters Anthony S. Phillips and Louis J. Matthews. We also join you in praying for the recovery of Lieutenant Charles Redding and fire fighter Joseph Morgan, Jr., from the injuries they suffered in Sunday's fire.

    These brave individuals and their fellow fire fighters across the country reflect the highest standards of community service, facing danger to save lives and protect property. The fire that claimed the lives of Anthony Phillips and Louis Matthews is a devastating reminder of the risks that every fire fighter confronts on a regular basis.

    Sacrificing all to safeguard the well-being of others, fire fighters Phillips and Matthews represent what is best about America. Their service and devotion will be long remembered by the people of Washington, D.C., and citizens across our nation.

    Hillary and I extend our deepest sympathy to the families and friends of these courageous fire fighters. We hope you can take comfort in remembering how they lived their lives and in the honor they brought to their noble profession. We are keeping all of you in our thoughts and prayers.

Bill Clinton

He Answered the Call

WYLIE COURTS FAMILY

13TH & I STREETS, N.E.
WASHINGTON, D.C. 20002

June 2, 1999

Family of Anthony Phillips:

It's always sorrowful to hear of the passing of one of our loved ones and to share in that sorrow with the family.

My God sustain you. Trust Him when doubt seems strong. Trust him when strength may be small. Trust Him when simply trusting Him may be the hardest thing of all.

Although no words can take away the sorrow that you bear, may it be comfort to know that others care and may the Father of us all whose mercies never cease sustain you in your hour of need.

The Kingdom of God is being prepared for you personally. The invitation from the Lord is to you personally, if lost, my friends. There will be no one to blame but you personally.

Behold, I stand at the door and knock. If any man hear my voice, and open the door I will come into him and sup with him and he with Me. (Rev. 3:20)

Blessed are they that do His commandments, that they may have right to the tree of life and may enter in through the gates into the city. (Rev. 22:14)

May the Father, God Creator of Heaven and Earth and all things therein renew your strength, spirit and give you inner peace and that his mercies never cease to sustain you in your hour of need.

We will continue to pray for you.

With Heartfelt Sympathy,
The Wylie Courts Residents

In Memory Of...

[Congressional Record (Bound Edition), Volume 145 (1999), Part 9]
[Extensions of Remarks]

[Page 12295]

[From the U.S. Government Publishing Office, www.gpo.gov]

IN MEMORY OF FIREFIGHTER ANTHONY PHILLIPS, ENGINE COMPANY NO. 10,

NATION'S CAPITAL

HON. ELEANOR HOLMES NORTON

of the district of columbia

in the house of representatives

Tuesday, June 8, 1999

Ms. NORTON. Mr. Speaker, in my conversation with Lysa Phillips, the very young widow of Firefighter Anthony Phillips, I have been struck by her personal strength and her inner peace. I have deeply admired how she has drawn on the strong bond and deep love she and Firefighter Phillips shared and the extraordinary devotion that Firefighter Phillips had for his children, his family, and his work. So strong was his love for his family, his God, and his work that his love has madeLysa and his family especially strong.

Again and again, we are told that Firefighter Phillips loved his work. We are indebted to brave young firefighters, like FirefigherPhillips, who love their work and who, unlike us, neither fear nor shun danger, but rush to conquer it. We give thanks for the young, loving life of Anthony Phillips and we honor him for his courage and his sacrifice.

In remembering Firefighter Phillips, we are especially mindful of the men and women of the Department he has left behind to carry on his work of confronting danger whenever and wherever it appears. To properly remember Firefighter Anthony Phillips is to remember the members of the District of Columbia Fire Dpartment and their indispensable mission,the debt we owe him, and the debt we owe them.

Closure!

www.ingramcontent.com/pod-product-compliance
Lightning Source LLC
Chambersburg PA
CBHW052030070526
44584CB00016B/1982